CALIFORNIA

DMV EXAM

WORKBOOK

400+ PRACTICE QUESTIONS TO NAVIGATE YOUR DMV EXAM WITH CONFIDENCE

CONTENT

INTRODUCTION

Welcome and thank you for choosing our workbook as your trusted companion on your journey to achieving your driver's license. This meticulously designed resource is not just a book, but a complete guide intended to empower you with the knowledge, confidence, and practice necessary to ace the DMV test.

This workbook is crafted with a careful selection of questions derived directly from the Driver's Manual of your respective state. Each question has been thoughtfully constructed to cover key areas of the exam, providing a comprehensive understanding of every aspect you'll be tested on. Our primary aim is to help you fully grasp the material, turning any uncertainties into strengths.

Here are some strategic steps to ensure you make the most of this valuable resource:

1. **Consistent Practice:** Begin by taking the practice tests in one sitting, from start to finish, replicating the actual exam conditions. This will not only test your knowledge but also build your endurance and help you manage time effectively.
2. **Detailed Review:** Post completion, focus on the questions you answered incorrectly. The answer key, located at the back of this book, provides clear explanations for each question. Understanding your mistakes is a critical part of the learning process and will significantly improve your performance.
3. **Regular Revision:** As the saying goes, "Repetition is the mother of learning." Regular revision will reinforce your knowledge and help you remember information for longer periods.
4. **Mock Exams:** Once you've thoroughly studied and revised the material, take the practice tests again. This time, aim for higher scores. Gradually, you will see your understanding deepen and your scores improve.
5. **Stay Updated:** Laws and regulations can change. It's crucial to ensure you're studying the most recent information. Check online resources or contact your local DMV for updates.

Remember, the journey to success lies in persistent and intelligent practice. The more you engage with the material, the better you will understand it, and the more comfortable you'll be during the actual DMV exam.

For every question in this workbook, you'll find a corresponding answer accompanied by a detailed explanation. In instances where multiple answers may seem correct, we've included a comprehensive explanation for each response. This approach will help you understand not only why the correct answer is indeed correct, but also why the other options are incorrect. This level of understanding is what separates those who merely pass from those who excel.

We believe that with dedication, practice, and the right guidance, anyone can master the skills required to pass the DMV test. This workbook is your map to that journey. Good luck on your path to becoming a confident and responsible driver!

THE CALIFORNIA DRIVER'S HANDBOOK

The CALIFORNIA Department of Motor Vehicles strongly recommends that all test takers familiarize themselves with the official manual. This comprehensive guide offers an in-depth understanding of the rules, regulations, and knowledge required to pass your exam. It is suggested that you read through this manual at least once to familiarize yourself with the necessary content.

To access this invaluable resource, simply scan the provided QR code or type the link into your browser to download it.

https://www.dmv.ca.gov/portal/driver-handbooks/

CHEAT SHEETS

In addition to the official handbook, we have included Cheat Sheets in this workbook. These are specifically designed to assist you in reviewing the top 100 questions commonly seen on the DMV written test. These Cheat Sheets serve as a quick reference guide and a powerful review tool, making them an indispensable resource in the days leading up to your exam. You will find them conveniently located at the end of the book, right before the Answer Sheets.

We wholeheartedly wish you the best of luck on your journey towards obtaining your driver's license. To maximize your chances of success, we encourage you to take our practice tests as many times as necessary. Remember, consistent practice is the key to mastery!

There's no time like the present. Start studying today and embark on your path to acing your DMV exam! We thank you once again for choosing this book as your trusted guide, and we hope it assists you in reaching your driving objectives.

As a final note, we would love to hear about your learning journey. Please consider writing a review of the book. Your feedback is invaluable in helping us refine our resources and better assist future drivers on their path to success.

BONUSES

THE TOP 100 MOST FAQs

Get access to our compilation of the 100 most commonly asked questions on the DMV exam. We strongly recommend you review this valuable resource prior to your test day, ensuring your readiness for the most likely questions to come your way! Keep in mind, the more you rehearse, the more refined your performance will be on the actual DMV test.

To retrieve this resource, simply enter the provided link into your browser or make use of the QR Code for swift access.

- https://dl.bookfunnel.com/lhf68zpx12

200 BONUS PRACTICE QUESTIONS

"Master the DMV: Bonus Practice Questions" is a comprehensive collection of additional, carefully crafted questions that mirror the variety, style, and complexity of the ones you'll encounter in the real DMV exam. Perhaps you've already completed the questions in our main guide and are yearning for more practice. Or maybe you just want to challenge yourself and ensure no stone is left unturned in your preparations. Regardless of your motivation, this bonus eBook is your perfect ally.

To retrieve this resource, simply enter the provided link into your browser or make use of the QR Code for swift access.

https://dl.bookfunnel.com/l15oxwpd9e

PRACTICE TEST 1

Gear up for the DMV driving permit test by engaging with practice questions that bear a striking resemblance (and are frequently identical!) to the ones you'll encounter on the actual DMV exam.

Total Questions: 40
Correct Answer to pass: 32

Question 1 - Practice Test 1

In the event of a skid, which is the most crucial tool for regaining control?

- ☐ The antilock braking system (ABS)
- ☐ The steering wheel
- ☐ The accelerator

Question 2 - Practice Test 1

If you are a California driver who is under 21 and get your first DUI conviction, your license will be suspended for a year and _____.

- ☐ you will need an adult in the car when driving
- ☐ you will have to retake the driving test
- ☐ you will need to attend a DUI program

Question 3 - Practice Test 1

A _____ on your side of the road signifies an area where overtaking is not permitted.

- ☐ A discontinuous yellow line
- ☐ A continuous yellow line
- ☐ A discontinuous white line

Question 4 - Practice Test 1

A driver who is under 21 years old

   ☐   can maintain a blood alcohol content of 0.04%

   ☐   should have a blood alcohol content of zero

   ☐   can maintain a blood alcohol content of 0.02%

Question 5 - Practice Test 1

Upon reaching an intersection with a through road but lacking stop signs or yield signs, you must

   ☐   make a quick turn to adjust to the through road's traffic speed

   ☐   speed up to merge with traffic

   ☐   yield to traffic and pedestrians on the through road

Question 6 - Practice Test 1

When you see a "speed zone ahead" sign, it indicates that you're approaching _____.

   ☐   an expressway or highway

   ☐   a zone with a reduced speed limit

   ☐   a zone where the speed limit should not exceed 75 mph

Question 7 - Practice Test 1

In California, a person under the age of ____ is not permitted to have a job that requires them to drive for compensation.

   ☐   17

   ☐   16

   ☐   18

Question 8 - Practice Test 1

If a California driver holding a provisional driver's license receives a traffic violation but neglects to pay the fine or appear in court, _____.

☐   his/her school will be informed

☐   his/her parents will be informed

☐   his/her license will be suspended

Question 9 - Practice Test 1

_____ typically, are diamond-shaped with yellow backgrounds and black lettering or symbols.

☐   Destination signs

☐   Warning signs

☐   Regulatory signs

Question 10 - Practice Test 1

If an underage California driver's preliminary alcohol screening (PAS) test shows a blood alcohol concentration (BAC) of _____ or higher, the officer might request a second test.

☐   0.04%

☐   0.05%

☐   0.03%

Question 11 - Practice Test 1

If a provisional license holder in California has been implicated in two accidents where they were at fault within their first year of holding the license, the action required is to _____.

☐   hand over the license to the DMV

☐   be accompanied while driving for a month

☐   pay a penalty

Question 12 - Practice Test 1

Your overall stopping distance includes your _____.

☐ perception distance, reaction distance, and braking distance

☐ distance of perception and reaction distance

☐ distance of perception, reaction distance, and deduction distance.

Question 13 - Practice Test 1

A minor in California can have their driver's license revoked at any time by _____.

☐ a school administrator

☐ a parent or legal guardian

☐ a medical professional

Question 14 - Practice Test 1

A minor who is driving receives a call on their cell phone. They must _____.

☐ avoid carrying a cell phone while driving

☐ employ a hands-free device to take the call

☐ avoid answering the call

Question 15 - Practice Test 1

For the initial 12 months after receiving a provisional driver's license in California, you are NOT permitted to drive alone _____.

☐ between 10:00 p.m. to 6:00 a.m

☐ between 11:00 p.m. to 5:00 a.m

☐ between 9:00 p.m. to 7:00 a.m

Question 16 - Practice Test 1

**A broken yellow line alongside a solid yellow line signifies that
_____.**

- ☐ passing is allowed on the side of the solid line, but not on the side of the broken line

- ☐ passing is forbidden on both sides

- ☐ passing is permitted on the side of the broken line, but not on the side of the solid line

Question 17 - Practice Test 1

If you are a driver below 21 years in California and are found guilty of alcohol consumption, your driver's license will be suspended for ____ year(s).

- ☐ 3

- ☐ 2

- ☐ 1

Question 18 - Practice Test 1

A written authorization can allow a driver with a provisional license in California to drive during prohibited hours _____.

- ☐ for medical treatment

- ☐ for school or work-related activities

- ☐ for any of the reasons mentioned above

Question 19 - Practice Test 1

Adverse weather like rain, snow, and ice diminish your visibility ahead, so to halt your vehicle safely, you should _____.

- ☐ increase your speed

- ☐ turn on high-beam headlights

- ☐ increase the distance you maintain from the vehicle in front

Question 20 - Practice Test 1

If you are 18 years or older and possess a California instruction permit, your driving should always be supervised by someone who _____.

- ☐ is at least 18 years old

- ☐ has a valid California driver's license

- ☐ fulfills both of the above requirements

Question 21 - Practice Test 1

Close to ____ of California drivers aged 15 to 19 receive at least one traffic violation conviction during their inaugural year of driving.

- ☐ 30%

- ☐ 10%

- ☐ 50%

Question 22 - Practice Test 1

Upon noticing a parked school bus with its red lights flashing, you should _____.

- ☐ drive at 10 mph and look out for children crossing

- ☐ slow down and proceed with caution

- ☐ halt and stay halted until the lights stop flashing

Question 23 - Practice Test 1

While driving on gravel or dirt, slowing down is crucial because _____.

☐   dirt may obscure the windshield

☐   traction is significantly reduced

☐   driving fast is uncomfortable

Question 24 - Practice Test 1

_____ are specifically designed to facilitate vehicles slowing down and exiting expressways.

☐   Exit ramps

☐   Acceleration lanes

☐   Roundabouts

Question 25 - Practice Test 1

Before switching lanes, ensuring no traffic is _____.

☐   behind your vehicle

☐   beside your vehicle

☐   both behind and beside your vehicle

Question 26 - Practice Test 1

For parking, making turns at low speeds, or recovering from skidding, you can use _____.

☐   the hand-to-hand steering technique

☐   the hand-over-hand steering technique

☐   the two-hand steering technique

Question 27 - Practice Test 1

You are behind a large truck signaling a right turn. You should anticipate _____.

- ☐ the truck abruptly stopping
- ☐ the truck turning close to the right curb
- ☐ the truck veering left

Question 28 - Practice Test 1

Typically, at the end of most freeway entrance ramps, you will encounter _____ which allows you to pick up speed.

- ☐ an acceleration lane
- ☐ a slow lane
- ☐ a deceleration lane

Question 29 - Practice Test 1

Under the laws of California, is it lawful to park in front of a driveway, either partially or fully obstructing it?

- ☐ No, never
- ☐ Only for a duration of 15 minutes or less
- ☐ Yes, if it is your own driveway

Question 30 - Practice Test 1

The driver of a vehicle being passed must _____ until the pass is completed.

- ☐ not increase speed
- ☐ stop
- ☐ shift to the left

Question 31 - Practice Test 1

Diversions that could potentially pull your focus from the road include

- [ ] interactions with your phone, such as texting or speaking
- [ ] constantly glancing at your mirrors
- [ ] checking your vehicle's blind spots

Question 32 - Practice Test 1

Upon spotting a loose animal on your driving path, you ought to _____.

- [ ] reduce your speed or halt, if it's safe
- [ ] sound your horn at the animal
- [ ] accelerate to swiftly pass the animal

Question 33 - Practice Test 1

A crosshatched area next to a designated disabled parking space _____.

- [ ] serves as a no parking zone
- [ ] acts as a rest area
- [ ] is a safe area to pull off the road

Question 34 - Practice Test 1

In the event that you're transporting a load extending more than 4 feet from your vehicle's rear bumper, what should you attach at the load's far end?

- ☐ One red or orange flag during the day and two red lights at night

- ☐ Two white flags during the day and two red lights at night

- ☐ One red or orange flag during the day and one red light at night

Question 35 - Practice Test 1

While sharing a road with a light-rail vehicle, _____.

- ☐ never occupy the lane adjacent to a light-rail vehicle

- ☐ never attempt a turn in front of an approaching light-rail vehicle

- ☐ trail the light-rail vehicle very closely

Question 36 - Practice Test 1

If you approach an intersection where the traffic signals are out of order, you must _____ before entering the intersection and then yield the right-of-way.

- ☐ come to a full stop

- ☐ speed up

- ☐ slow down

Question 37 - Practice Test 1

In California, you are NOT allowed to halt at a _____ curb to pick up or drop off passengers.

☐ white

☐ yellow

☐ red

Question 38 - Practice Test 1

If you want to transport your dog in the back of your pickup truck, the dog must be _____.

☐ adequately restrained

☐ supplied with sufficient food and water

☐ protected from sun exposure

Question 39 - Practice Test 1

If you are pulling a trailer on a divided highway in California with at least four lanes in your direction, which lanes can you use?

☐ Any lane except the farthest left lane

☐ Only the farthest right lane

☐ Only the two farthest right lanes

Question 40 - Practice Test 1

When following a vehicle at night, you should always _____.

☐ dim your high-beam headlights

☐ switch off your headlights

☐ use your high-beam headlights

PRACTICE TEST 2

Gear up for the DMV driving permit test by engaging with practice questions that bear a striking resemblance (and are frequently identical!) to the ones you'll encounter on the actual DMV exam.

Total Questions: 40
Correct Answer to pass: 32

Question 1 - Practice Test 2

In the event that your vehicle breaks down on train tracks with a train approaching, what is the appropriate course of action?

☐   Alert the train by opening your doors and signaling

☐   Quickly evacuate the vehicle and move a safe distance away

☐   Attempt to restart the engine

☐   Make an effort to push the vehicle off the tracks

Question 2 - Practice Test 2

What should you do if another driver is tailgating you?

☐   Shift into the left lane

☐   Gradually decrease your speed and pull off the road if needed

☐   Speed up

☐   Brake to dissuade the tailgater

Question 3 - Practice Test 2

When double solid lines are present next to your lane, it means you are:

☐ Not permitted to pass or change lanes

☐ Permitted to pass

☐ Allowed to change lanes

☐ Allowed to make a turn

Question 4 - Practice Test 2

In heavy rain, your car's tires can lose contact with the road by riding on a layer of water. This is known as:

☐ Waterplaning

☐ Rainplaning

☐ Frictionplaning

☐ Hydroplaning

Question 5 - Practice Test 2

Typically, _____ are diamond-shaped with black letters or symbols on a yellow background.

☐ Warning signs

☐ Service signs

☐ Regulatory signs

☐ Destination signs

Question 6 - Practice Test 2

When the road is _____, you should reduce your speed by half.

- ☐ slippery
- ☐ wet
- ☐ packed with snow
- ☐ none of the above

Question 7 - Practice Test 2

When faced with an aggressive driver, you should:

- ☐ Engage in calling names
- ☐ Exit your vehicle
- ☐ Make rude gestures
- ☐ Avoid eye contact

Question 8 - Practice Test 2

In the event of a tire blowout while driving, you should:

- ☐ Accelerate
- ☐ Brake forcefully
- ☐ Shift to a higher gear
- ☐ Grip the steering wheel tightly

Question 9 - Practice Test 2

At an intersection, a solid yellow traffic light signifies that you should:

- ☐ Accelerate to pass the signal before it turns red
- ☐ Slow down and proceed with caution
- ☐ Maintain your current speed
- ☐ Prepare to stop for a red light

Question 10 - Practice Test 2

If your vehicle's rear wheels begin to skid, what should you do?

☐   Steer the wheel to the left

☐   Steer the wheel in the direction of the skid

☐   Steer the wheel opposite the skid

☐   Steer the wheel to the right

Question 11 - Practice Test 2

When two vehicles approach an intersection from opposite directions at roughly the same time, _____.

☐   the left-turning vehicle must yield to the vehicle going straight or turning right

☐   the vehicle with more passengers should go first

☐   the vehicle on the right must yield to the vehicle on the left

☐   the right-turning vehicle must yield to the left-turning vehicle

Question 12 - Practice Test 2

To maintain an appropriate space cushion between your vehicle and the one ahead, apply the:

☐   Three-second rule

☐   Two-second rule

☐   Four-second rule

☐   One-second rule

Question 13 - Practice Test 2

When entering a roundabout, rotary, or traffic circle, you must yield the right-of-way to:

- ☐ Pedestrians
- ☐ Both pedestrians and vehicles already in the circle
- ☐ Vehicles in the circle
- ☐ Nobody

Question 14 - Practice Test 2

Two-thirds of all deer-vehicle collisions occur during which of the following months?

- ☐ January, February, and March
- ☐ October, November, and December
- ☐ March, April, and May
- ☐ June, July, and August

Question 15 - Practice Test 2

For improved visibility in fog, rain, or snow, use:

- ☐ Emergency lights
- ☐ Low-beam headlights
- ☐ High-beam headlights
- ☐ Interior lights

Question 16 - Practice Test 2

You shall not pass a vehicle on the left if:

☐ Your lane has a broken white line

☐ Your lane has a solid yellow center line

☐ You are far away from a curve

☐ Your lane has a broken yellow line

Question 17 - Practice Test 2

_____ enable vehicles to exit expressways.

☐ Exit ramps

☐ Turnpikes

☐ Acceleration lanes

☐ Roundabouts

Question 18 - Practice Test 2

To perform a turnaround on a narrow, two-way street, execute:

☐ Single-point turn

☐ Two-point turn

☐ Four-point turn

☐ Three-point turn

Question 19 - Practice Test 2

Even ____ alcoholic drink(s) can impact your ability to drive safely.

☐ three

☐ four

☐ one

☐ two

Question 20 - Practice Test 2

When another vehicle passes you on the left, you should _____ until the vehicle has safely overtaken you.

- ☐　　pull over and stop
- ☐　　accelerate and keep to the right
- ☐　　slow down and stay to the left
- ☐　　slow down and stay centered in your lane

Question 21 - Practice Test 2

When turning right on a multi-lane road, which lane should you typically use?

- ☐　　Any lane
- ☐　　The leftmost lane
- ☐　　A middle lane
- ☐　　The rightmost lane

Question 22 - Practice Test 2

What should you do when an emergency vehicle with flashing lights, a siren, or an air horn is approaching you from any direction?

- ☐　　Change lanes and maintain the same speed
- ☐　　Pull over to the right and stop
- ☐　　Decelerate and move into the left lane
- ☐　　Accelerate and clear the lane

Question 23 - Practice Test 2

At a railroad crossing, what do flashing red lights, lowered crossing gates, or ringing bells indicate?

☐ A train has just passed

☐ A lane change is necessary

☐ You must stop at least 15 feet from the railroad tracks

☐ Slow down and proceed with caution

Question 24 - Practice Test 2

When is it prohibited to pass a vehicle on the right?

☐ When the vehicle is making a left turn

☐ When the vehicle is going straight

☐ When the vehicle is making a right turn

☐ When the vehicle is on a one-way road with two lanes of traffic

Question 25 - Practice Test 2

In open country at night, which headlights should you use?

☐ High-beam headlights

☐ Parking lights

☐ Low-beam headlights

☐ None of the above

Question 26 - Practice Test 2

Where can crosswalks be found?

☐ Only on multi-lane roads

☐ Regardless of whether there are crosswalk lines

☐ Only in residential areas

☐ Only where there are line markings

Question 27 - Practice Test 2

Due to their size, tractor-trailers often appear to be _____.

☐ moving faster

☐ moving backward

☐ moving dangerously

☐ moving slower

Question 28 - Practice Test 2

At which locations should you always look both ways?

☐ Railroad crossings

☐ Crosswalks

☐ Intersections

☐ All of the above

Question 29 - Practice Test 2

When is it necessary to signal before passing another vehicle?

- ☐ Always
- ☐ Only if there are vehicles directly behind you
- ☐ If the driver of the vehicle may be unaware of your intention to pass
- ☐ On expressways with more than two lanes

Question 30 - Practice Test 2

When is it appropriate to use your horn?

- ☐ To warn pedestrians or other drivers of potential danger
- ☐ To encourage other drivers to drive faster
- ☐ To inform another driver of their mistake
- ☐ To tell pedestrians to get off the road

Question 31 - Practice Test 2

Which factor does not influence your blood alcohol concentration (BAC)?

- ☐ Time between drinks
- ☐ Your body weight
- ☐ Time since your last drink
- ☐ Type of alcohol consumed

Question 32 - Practice Test 2

Who is responsible for ensuring a child in the vehicle you're driving is properly restrained?

☐ The vehicle owner

☐ The child

☐ Yourself

☐ The child's parents

Question 33 - Practice Test 2

If a driver's left arm is extended out the window and bent upward, this indicates they intend to _____.

☐ proceed straight

☐ slow down or stop

☐ turn right

☐ turn left

Question 34 - Practice Test 2

A flashing red light signifies _____.

☐ caution

☐ slowing down

☐ the same as a stop sign

☐ the same as a yield sign

Question 35 - Practice Test 2

In freezing temperatures, which areas are most likely to ice over first?

- ☐ Bridges and overpasses
- ☐ Residential streets
- ☐ Tunnels
- ☐ Gravel roads

Question 36 - Practice Test 2

When a vehicle merges onto an expressway, who has the right-of-way?

- ☐ The merging vehicle
- ☐ The fastest vehicle
- ☐ Vehicles already on the expressway
- ☐ The slowest vehicle

Question 37 - Practice Test 2

If an emergency vehicle with flashing lights or a siren approaches, you must immediately pull over and stop unless _____.

- ☐ there is adequate space in another lane for it
- ☐ you are in a hurry
- ☐ you have entered a school zone
- ☐ you are in an intersection

Question 38 - Practice Test 2

You are the third vehicle to arrive at a four-way stop at different times. Which vehicle has the right-of-way?

☐   The vehicle that is not signaling

☐   The vehicle turning right

☐   The vehicle that arrived first

☐   The vehicle to your right

Question 39 - Practice Test 2

You approach a crosswalk with a pedestrian and guide dog attempting to cross the street. What should you do?

☐   Tell the pedestrian it is safe to cross

☐   Stop and turn off your engine

☐   Wait for the pedestrian to cross the street

☐   Honk your horn to indicate it is safe to cross

Question 40 - Practice Test 2

When can you safely merge back in front of a vehicle you just passed?

☐   When the driver honks to let you in

☐   When you see the entire front bumper of the passed vehicle in your rear-view mirror

☐   When you make direct eye contact with the driver in your rearview mirror.

☐   When you can't see the passing vehicle via the window.

ROAD SIGNS

In the United States, the trend is moving towards using symbols instead of words on road signs for more effective communication. These symbols break down language barriers and facilitate immediate understanding, quickly becoming the global norm for traffic control devices.

It's imperative for all drivers to be well-versed with these traffic sign symbols to ensure the smooth functioning and safety of our transportation networks.

Don't worry, we've got your back. Our resource includes over 100 questions focused on Road Signs to help you master this vital aspect.

Total Questions: 100
Correct Answer to pass: 80

Question 1 - Road Signs

What does this image represent?

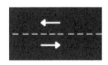

- ☐ When the way ahead is clear, passing on the left is permitted
- ☐ Passing on the right is not permitted
- ☐ Passing is prohibited in both directions
- ☐ Passing is only permitted during night

Question 2 - Road Signs

What exactly does this road sign mean?

    ☐   A construction zone is ahead

    ☐   There is a parking area ahead

    ☐   There is a forest zone is ahead

    ☐   There's a rest stop ahead

Question 3 - Road Signs

What does this image represent?

    ☐   A child care center

    ☐   T-intersection ahead

    ☐   Playground ahead

    ☐   School zone ahead

Question 4 - Road Signs

What does this sign denote?

○   A side street near a railroad crossing

○   A bridge

○   A Truck service center

○   A pedestrian underpass

Question 5 - Road Signs

This symbol denotes

○   a hospital zone

○   wheelchair accessibility

○   a parking area for the handicapped

○   a pedestrian crosswalk

Question 6 - Road Signs

This orange triangular reflective sign indicates

☐   a vehicle that moves in a rapid pace

☐   a vehicle transporting hazardous materials

☐   a vehicle that moves slowly

☐   a truck

Question 7 - Road Signs

Which of these signs points you in the direction of a hospital?

A   B   C   D

☐   C

☐   B

☐   A

☐   D

Question 8 - Road Signs

What does this sign indicate?

- ☐   Do not accelerate to 45 mph
- ☐   Drive at a 45-mph speed
- ☐   There is a speed zone is ahead; prepare to slow down to 45 mph
- ☐   Construction zone ahead

Question 9 - Road Signs

Typically, a vertical rectangular traffic sign gives

- ☐   instructions to the driver
- ☐   directions to the driver to come to a halt
- ☐   a warning about the construction work
- ☐   a warning about the road's condition

Question 10 - Road Signs

This symbol denotes

☐   a lane for turning left

☐   a diversion

☐   that the road ahead curves to the left

☐   a lane for turning right

Question 11 - Road Signs

This symbol indicates

☐   railroad crossing

☐   road work

☐   a right turn

☐   road maintenance

Question 12 - Road Signs

What is the significance of this flashing arrow panel?

- ☐   The lane ahead of you has been closed
- ☐   The lane ahead is open for traffic
- ☐   Flaggers are in front
- ☐   There are right lane curves ahead

Question 13 - Road Signs

What does this sign indicate?

- ☐   A divided highway begins ahead
- ☐   One-way traffic ahead
- ☐   The divided highway ends ahead
- ☐   Merging Traffic

Question 14 - Road Signs

What is the meaning of this sign?

- ☐   When the green arrow is ON, left turns are permitted
- ☐   When the steady green signal is lit and there are no oncoming vehicles, left turns are permitted
- ☐   When the green arrow goes out, no left turns are permitted
- ☐   Left turns are only permitted when the steady green signal is OFF

Question 15 - Road Signs

What exactly does this sign mean?

- ☐   There is disabled parking ahead.
- ☐   There is a disabled crossing ahead.
- ☐   A hospital is on the way.
- ☐   There is a pedestrian crosswalk ahead.

Question 16 - Road Signs

This warning sign informs drivers that

◻   a single-use path crossing ahead

◻   there is a school zone ahead

◻   it is a bicycle lane

◻   a multi-use path crossing is ahead

Question 17 - Road Signs

This symbol indicates that

◻   bicyclists should only ride in the lane designated by the sign

◻   there is a bikeway crosses the road ahead

◻   bicyclists are not allowed to use this lane

◻   there is a no-passing zone for bicyclists ahead

Question 18 - Road Signs

If you see this sign while driving in the left lane, what should you do?

- ☐ continue straight
- ☐ merge into the right lane
- ☐ turn left
- ☐ turn right

Question 19 - Road Signs

This warning sign indicates

- ☐ there will be sharp right and left turns
- ☐ the road ahead takes a left turn
- ☐ a winding road
- ☐ that the road ahead bends to the right, then to the left

Question 20 - Road Signs

What does this signal indicate at an intersection?

☐   Pedestrians are not allowed to enter the crosswalk

☐   Drivers must slow down

☐   Pedestrians who are already in the crosswalk may finish their crossing

☐   Pedestrians are permitted to enter the crosswalk

Question 21 - Road Signs

What does this symbol indicate?

☐   A hospital ahead

☐   There is a rest stop ahead

☐   High school ahead

☐   Handicapped service

Question 22 - Road Signs

This symbol indicates

☐   the exit number 117 is up ahead

☐   next available exit is 117 miles away

☐   to enter the Route 117, take this exit

☐   none of the above

Question 23 - Road Signs

This sign indicates the location of

☐   a gas station

☐   a handicapped service

☐   a rest zone

☐   a hospital zone

Question 24 - Road Signs

What does this sign mean?

☐   Speed limit ahead

☐   Speed restriction on-ramp

☐   Speed advisory at roundabout

☐   An exit speed restriction

Question 25 - Road Signs

What exactly does this sign mean?

☐   Only left turns are permitted

☐   Traffic must merge to the right

☐   Traffic must merge to the left

☐   Only right turns are permitted

Question 26 - Road Signs

What exactly does this sign mean?

☐   You shouldn't take a right turn

☐   You must not take a left turn

☐   This section of the road is closed

☐   Do not merge

Question 27 - Road Signs

What exactly does this sign mean?

☐   A hospital zone

☐   Telephone service available ahead

☐   Gas station ahead

☐   There will be a rest zone ahead

Question 28 - Road Signs

What exactly does this sign indicate?

□   You are about to approach a left turn

□   You are about to approach a right turn

□   A sharp U-turn

□   A sharp left turn ahead

Question 29 - Road Signs

What should you do if you see this road sign?

□   Exit the highway at a speed of at least 30 miles per hour

□   Exit the highway at a speed of no more than 30 miles per hour

□   Increase your speed to 30 mph to pass the vehicle in front of you

□   Exit the freeway at a top speed of 60 mph

Question 30 - Road Signs

This pavement markings in this image indicate that

☐ It is not allowed to pass

☐ You can pass if it is safe

☐ Take a detour

☐ Make a U turn

Question 31 - Road Signs

What is the meaning of this traffic sign?

☐ It is not permissible to pass a vehicle on the left

☐ Only left turns are allowed

☐ Passing is legal in these directions

☐ Only move in the indicated directions

Question 32 - Road Signs

What does this sign mean?

- ☐ Hospital Zone
- ☐ You are approaching a A four-way intersection
- ☐ A side road is ahead
- ☐ A railroad crossing is ahead

Question 33 - Road Signs

What does this symbol indicate?

- ☐ Railroad crossing with low ground clearance
- ☐ Railroad crossing that is closed
- ☐ Railroad crossing that is being repaired
- ☐ Byway near a railroad crossing

Question 34 - Road Signs

What does this image mean?

□   A broken white line that forbids passing

□   A broken white line that permits passing

□   An accident occurred

□   The vehicle is making a U-turn

Question 35 - Road Signs

This is an octagonal (eight-sided) figure which indicates

□   a Yield symbol

□   Do Not Enter sign

□   a Stop sign

□   a Construction sign

Question 36 - Road Signs

You can find this orange sign at

- ☐ railroad crossings
- ☐ the intersections that are uncontrolled
- ☐ school zones
- ☐ work zones

Question 37 - Road Signs

What does this sign indicate?

- ☐ A winding road
- ☐ A curve ahead
- ☐ A slippery road
- ☐ A two-way road

Question 38 - Road Signs

What does this sign denote?

☐ A winding road awaits; drivers should follow the signs

☐ A gravel road ahead with sharp curves; drivers must proceed with caution

☐ When the road is wet, it becomes slippery; proceed cautiously

☐ A sharp curve near a hill; vehicles must proceed cautiously

Question 39 - Road Signs

What does this sign indicate?

☐ "Right Lane Ends"

☐ Freeway interchange

☐ Sharp turn on a highway

☐ Beginning of a Divided Highway

Question 40 - Road Signs

What does this sign indicate?

☐   You are not permitted to park on both sides of the sign

☐   You can park on the left side of the sign

☐   Parking is available to the right of the sign

☐   You are not allowed to park to the left of the sign

Question 41 - Road Signs

What does this sign mean?

☐   The divided highway ends

☐   A divided highway begins ahead

☐   There's an underpass ahead

☐   Right lane is closed

Question 42 - Road Signs

This sign means that you are

☐   in a wrong lane

☐   driving in the wrong direction

☐   In the city

☐   moving in a bicycle lane

Question 43 - Road Signs

What exactly does this sign mean?

☐   Take Route 45

☐   The top speed is 45 miles per hour any time

☐   The minimum speed limit is 45 miles per hour

☐   The maximum speed limit at night is 45 mph

Question 44 - Road Signs

What exactly does this sign indicate?

- ☐ Emergency vehicles may enter the roadway
- ☐ Trucks transporting dangerous materials may enter the road
- ☐ Heavy vehicles may enter the road
- ☐ Farm vehicles may enter the roadway

Question 45 - Road Signs

What should you do if you come across this sign at an intersection?

- ☐ Do not move further
- ☐ Continue right
- ☐ Allow oncoming traffic to pass
- ☐ Before turning right or left, yield the right-of-way or stop

Question 46 - Road Signs

What exactly does this sign indicate?

- ☐ At the sign, all vehicles must make a U-turn
- ☐ U-turns are not permitted for trucks
- ☐ Vehicles are not permitted to make a U-turn at the sign
- ☐ It denotes none of the preceding

Question 47 - Road Signs

What does this sign mean?

- ☐ A side road is ahead
- ☐ A T-intersection is ahead; yield to cross traffic
- ☐ A four-way stop ahead; prepare to yield
- ☐ A tourist information center is ahead

Question 48 - Road Signs

What exactly does this sign mean?

☐   A deer crossing ahead

☐   Cattle crossing ahead

☐   Forest zone

☐   A zoo ahead

Question 49 - Road Signs

What does this sign indicate?

☐   The maximum allowable speed in a school zone

☐   The minimum allowable speed in a school zone

☐   When there are children present in a school zone, this is the maximum allowable speed

☐   When there are children present in a school zone, this is the minimum allowable speed

Question 50 - Road Signs

What does this sign mean?

☐ Parking available

☐ Lodging available

☐ Hospital service available

☐ Handicapped service area available

Question 51 - Road Signs

What exactly does this regulatory sign mean?

☐ The indicated lane is for high-occupancy vehicles during the hours mentioned

☐ At specific times, high-occupancy vehicles are prohibited

☐ Cars and buses are not permitted during the designated times

☐ The indicated lane is only for heavy vehicles

Question 52 - Road Signs

What does a stop sign accompanied by this sign (4-way) at an intersection indicate?

- ☐ For four seconds, you must come to stop
- ☐ There are four lanes of traffic
- ☐ Vehicles arriving from all four directions are required to yield
- ☐ Vehicles approaching the intersection from all four directions must stop

Question 53 - Road Signs

What exactly does this sign denote?

- ☐ The road is closed
- ☐ This road comes to an end at a T-intersection
- ☐ Narrow bridge's rails ahead
- ☐ A Y-intersection ahead

Question 54 - Road Signs

What does this symbol indicate?

- ☐ To get onto Route 47 north, make a right turn
- ☐ Route 47 north has one-way traffic
- ☐ Route 47 north begins here
- ☐ Route 47 comes to an end

Question 55 - Road Signs

What exactly does this sign indicate?

- ☐ RC flying zone ahead
- ☐ You're getting close to an airport
- ☐ Planes fly at low altitudes in that place
- ☐ Direction in which planes fly

Question 56 - Road Signs

What does this highway sign indicate?

☐   There is an upcoming side road

☐   There is an upcoming three-way stop

☐   There is a railroad crossing ahead

☐   There is a limited-access side road

Question 57 - Road Signs

This symbol denotes _____.

☐   a U Turn

☐   a sharp turn

☐   an emergency halt

☐   a right turn

Question 58 - Road Signs

What exactly does this sign mean?

- ☐ Speed limit on hills
- ☐ Speed limit at roundabouts
- ☐ Interstate route symbol
- ☐ A speed limit sign on expressways

Question 59 - Road Signs

What does this stop sign mean?

- ☐ Within 1,000 feet, there will be construction
- ☐ After 1,000 feet, turning right is banned
- ☐ An alternate route is 1,000 feet ahead
- ☐ There will be a parking zone ahead

Question 60 - Road Signs

What does this symbol indicate?

- ☐ A median
- ☐ There is a bump in the road ahead.
- ☐ A steep incline
- ☐ The road ahead is closed

Question 61 - Road Signs

What do this single broken (dashed) white line in the image denote?

- ☐ Traffic will be moving in the opposing directions
- ☐ Traffic moving in the same direction
- ☐ The road's shoulder
- ☐ Passing not allowed

Question 62 - Road Signs

What does this sign denote?

- ☐ School area
- ☐ Construction zone
- ☐ Road crew at work
- ☐ Pedestrian crosswalk

Question 63 - Road Signs

What does this warning sign mean?

- ☐ A stop sign ahead
- ☐ A yield sign
- ☐ Take a detour
- ☐ Slow-moving vehicles should follow directions

Question 64 - Road Signs

This sign warns drivers about

- ☐ students bus stop
- ☐ play zone for children
- ☐ school zone
- ☐ the pedestrian crosswalks

Question 65 - Road Signs

What does this regulatory sign indicate?

- ☐ Merge to the left
- ☐ Take right turn
- ☐ Do not take right turn
- ☐ Turning left is not allowed

Question 66 - Road Signs

What does the number depicted in this sign board stands for?

    ☐   A sign indicating a U.S. route marker

    ☐   An exit number

    ☐   Miles from the exit

    ☐   Speed limit on the exit ramp

Question 67 - Road Signs

This sign alerts drivers that they

    ☐   should not leave the pavement

    ☐   must extend their following distance to 6 seconds

    ☐   should move fast

    ☐   should move onto the shoulder

Question 68 - Road Signs

What exactly does this sign mean?

- ☐ Keep left of the divider
- ☐ You are getting close to a divided highway
- ☐ Take a detour
- ☐ Keep right of the divider

Question 69 - Road Signs

What exactly does this sign mean?

- ☐ You are not allowed to drive on the railroad tracks
- ☐ A railroad crossing
- ☐ You can drive on the railroad tracks.
- ☐ You must stop

Question 70 - Road Signs

What exactly does this sign mean?

- ☐ No vehicles should pass
- ☐ Slow down
- ☐ Stop for the pedestrians to cross
- ☐ Pedestrians are not allowed to cross

Question 71 - Road Signs

What do these pavement markings denote?

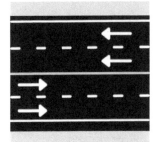

- ☐ Except for left turns, vehicles must not cross the solid yellow line
- ☐ Except for passing, vehicles must not cross the solid yellow line
- ☐ Under no circumstances may a vehicle cross the broken white lines
- ☐ None of the aforementioned

Question 72 - Road Signs

What exactly does this sign indicate?

☐   Stop immediately

☐   Pedestrian zone

☐   Turn right

☐   Flag person ahead

Question 73 - Road Signs

What does this sign indicate?

☐   Traffic is merging ahead

☐   A divided highway ahead

☐   Two-way road

☐   A narrow lane

Question 74 - Road Signs

What exactly does this sign denote?

☐   Narrow bridge ahead

☐   Acceleration lane ahead

☐   Huge traffic is ahead

☐   Narrow road ahead

Question 75 - Road Signs

What does this sign mean?

☐   The left lane comes to an end ahead

☐   The right lane comes to an end ahead

☐   A one-way road is ahead

☐   A narrow bridge ahead

Question 76 - Road Signs

You may travel in the lane indicated by this sign, _____.

- ☐ only if you're on a bicycle
- ☐ if you're passing the vehicle in front of you
- ☐ if you're on a motorcycle
- ☐ if you're transporting two or more people

Question 77 - Road Signs

What exactly is the meaning of this sign?

- ☐ There is a Y-intersection ahead
- ☐ Side road ahead.
- ☐ A hostel ahead
- ☐ Yield

Question 78 - Road Signs

What does this symbol denote?

- ☐ Speed limit on the interstate highway
- ☐ Distance between the current and the next exit
- ☐ The exit number
- ☐ Interstate highway number

Question 79 - Road Signs

This sign indicates that the parking spaces are for

- ☐ senior citizens
- ☐ bike riders
- ☐ the people with disabilities
- ☐ students

Question 80 - Road Signs

What exactly does this road sign mean?

- ☐ There is a farmhouse on the way
- ☐ A cattle crossing
- ☐ A veterinary hospital ahead
- ☐ There is a zoo ahead

Question 81 - Road Signs

What does this sign mean?

- ☐ Stopping or standing is not allowed
- ☐ A tunnel awaits you ahead
- ☐ It is not permitted to hitchhike
- ☐ You're almost to a school zone

Question 82 - Road Signs

What does this sign denote?

☐   The maximum number of vehicles that can park

☐   The maximum speed allowed on a road.

☐   A stopping place

☐   A sign indicating a United States route marking

Question 83 - Road Signs

What does this figure denote?

☐   A flag person is ahead

☐   Road crew is on the job

☐   There is a pedestrian crossing ahead; vehicles must yield.

☐   A school crossing is ahead; vehicles must move slowly

Question 84 - Road Signs

The availability of_____ is represented by this blue sign.

☐   Food

☐   Rest Area

☐   Gas station

☐   Hospital

Question 85 - Road Signs

If you see this sign and are travelling slower than the majority of traffic, what should you do?

☐   Increase your speed

☐   Enter the left lane

☐   Move to the right lane

☐   Take the next exit

Question 86 - Road Signs

What does the arrow on this sign indicate?

☐　　Drivers can choose to proceed in either way

☐　　Traffic must only travel in the direction indicated by the arrow

☐　　The lane ahead is reserved for right-turning trucks

☐　　All cars must come to a complete stop before making a right turn

Question 87 - Road Signs

What exactly does this sign mean?

☐　　A left turn is ahead of you

☐　　It is not permissible to turn left

☐　　You will encounter a sequence of curves ahead

☐　　There is a side road is entering from the right

Question 88 - Road Signs

What do these two arrows represent?

☐ Divided highway starts

☐ Divided highway ends

☐ Two-way traffic ahead

☐ Traffic may flow on both sides

Question 89 - Road Signs

What does this symbol indicate?

☐ Vehicles must go at a minimum of 40 miles per hour

☐ Slow-moving vehicles are not permitted to travel faster than 40 mph

☐ Vehicles should not exceed the posted speed restriction of 40 mph

☐ Vehicles must go at no more than 40 miles per hour

Question 90 - Road Signs

What exactly does this sign indicate?

☐   A work zone will be ahead of you

☐   There will be a bend on the way

☐   The road ahead will have a low point

☐   There will be a diversion ahead

Question 91 - Road Signs

For what purpose is this symbol used for?

☐   indicating the presence of a hospital

☐   displaying alternate routes in the event of road closures or construction

☐   Showing the designated routes

☐   Showing tourist routes

Question 92 - Road Signs

Which of the following pavement markings separates two lanes of traffic travelling in the same direction?

A   B   C

☐   B

☐   A

☐   C

☐   None of the preceding

Question 93 - Road Signs

What does this sign mean?

☐   Take neither a left nor a straight path

☐   Keep going straight

☐   Merge to the left

☐   Turn left or keep going straight

Question 94 - Road Signs

What exactly does this sign mean?

☐   Road permanently closed

☐   Handicapped Parking

☐   Parking is not permitted

☐   No U-turns

Question 95 - Road Signs

What exactly does this sign indicate?

☐   Change lanes

☐   Proceed straight

☐   Stop

☐   Take Left

Question 96 - Road Signs

What exactly do these yellow pavement markings indicate?

- ☐ Three-way intersection
- ☐ Right turns are permitted for vehicles travelling in either direction
- ☐ Left turns are permitted for vehicles travelling in either direction
- ☐ One-way street

Question 97 - Road Signs

What symbol is this?

- ☐ A stop sign
- ☐ A yield symbol
- ☐ Do Not Enter
- ☐ Work zone

Question 98 - Road Signs

What exactly does this sign mean?

- ☐ This lane permits you to turn left
- ☐ From this lane, you must make a U-turn
- ☐ You must detour at the intersection
- ☐ You have the option of making a U-turn from this lane

Question 99 - Road Signs

What does this sign mean?

- ☐ Getting close to exit 444
- ☐ You're 444 miles from the state line and the end of the road
- ☐ Arrived at Route 444
- ☐ None of the preceding

What does this signal indicate?

☐   You've arrived at an abandoned railroad track.

☐   You've arrived at a railroad crossing.

☐   There is a railroad track parallel to the road ahead.

☐   You've arrived at a train station.

SITUATIONS AND SIGNS

Presented here is a comprehensive assortment of Signage and Scenarios specifically designed to enhance your understanding of intersections and shared lanes. This collection is not just an assortment of random signs and situations but a carefully curated set of content meant to address all possible scenarios you may encounter on the road.

Total Questions: 25
Correct Answer to pass: 20

Question 1 - Signs and Situations

You notice a yellow "X" light flashing above your lane. What does it imply?

☐   You should exit this lane as soon as possible

☐   This lane is now closed

☐   This lane is clear

☐   This lane is only for turning left

Question 2 - Signs and Situations

You've come to halt 20 feet behind a school bus with flashing red lights. When will you be able to pass it?

☐   When it begins to move

☐   If a traffic officer waves you through

☐   If the bus driver waves you through

☐   All of the above

Question 3 - Signs and Situations

You notice a lane with white diamonds painted on it. What do they imply?

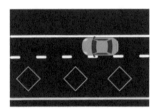

☐   This is a bus only lane

☐   This is a stop lane for emergencies

☐   This lane is now closed

☐   This is a reserved lane

Question 4 - Signs and Situations

At around the same moment, two cars arrive at an intersection. Which of the following statements is correct?

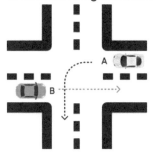

- ☐   All vehicles turning left must yield to Car B
- ☐   The drivers must select who will drive first
- ☐   Car A must yield since it is making a left turn
- ☐   None of the preceding statements are correct

Question 5 - Signs and Situations

You've parked facing a steep downhill slope. Which of the following actions should you take?

- ☐   If you have a manual transmission, keep it in reverse
- ☐   If you have a manual transmission, keep it in first gear
- ☐   If you have an automatic transmission, keep it in first gear
- ☐   If you have an automatic transmission, keep it in reverse

Question 6 - Signs and Situations

Three vehicles reach an intersection simultaneously. Who has the right-of-way?

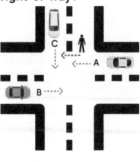

- ☐ Vehicle B
- ☐ Vehicle A
- ☐ The pedestrian
- ☐ Vehicle C

Question 7 - Signs and Situations

An emergency vehicle with flashing lights is stopped up ahead. What should you do?

- ☐ Accelerate and pass the emergency vehicle as quickly as possible
- ☐ Slow down; also, change to a non-adjacent lane if possible
- ☐ Change to a non-adjacent lane if possible; otherwise, slow down
- ☐ Proceed with the same pace

Question 8 - Signs and Situations

You have parked uphill on a steep incline. What should you do?

- ☐ Set your automatic transmission to first gear
- ☐ Set your automatic transmission to reverse
- ☐ Set your manual transmission to first gear
- ☐ Set your manual transmission to reverse

Question 9 - Signs and Situations

Which of the following takes priority (i.e., should be obeyed above all the others)?

- ☐ A red traffic light
- ☐ A traffic officer
- ☐ A stopped school bus with flashing red lights
- ☐ A warning road sign

Question 10 - Signs and Situations

What should you do when you see a flashing red light?

- ☐ You are not required to stop or yield at a flashing red signal
- ☐ When it is safe to do so, stop, yield, and then proceed
- ☐ Proceed with caution because the traffic signal is out
- ☐ Stop and hold your breath until the light turns green

Question 11 - Signs and Situations

You approach a railroad crossing with flashing red lights and a signal bell. A train is visible. Which of the following is correct?

☐   (a) You must stop at least 15 feet from the tracks

☐   (b) You can cross the tracks as soon as the train passed

☐   Both (a) and (b) are correct

☐   Neither (a) nor (b) is correct

Question 12 - Signs and Situations

You approach an intersection and notice a certain sign. What are your options?

☐   Stop completely and yield to traffic before proceeding

☐   Stop completely and then proceed

☐   Find another route; you cannot proceed through here

☐   Slow down and only proceed if the intersection is clear

Question 13 - Signs and Situations

When can you drive in a lane with this sign?

☐   When there is at least one passenger

☐   Whenever you want

☐   When at least two passengers are aboard

☐   Never (this is a bus and truck lane)

Question 14 - Signs and Situations

At at the same moment, two cars arrive at an uncontrolled intersection (one that is not controlled by signs or signals). Which of the following statements is correct?

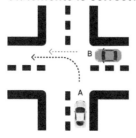

☐   Car A must yield because it is to the left of Car B

☐   Car B must yield because it is traveling straight through the intersection

☐   Car B must yield because it is on Car A's right

☐   None of the preceding statements are correct

Question 15 - Signs and Situations

You approach a crossroad with a green light and wish to drive straight through the intersection. Which of the following is correct?

☐ You are unable to proceed

☐ You are free to continue

☐ You may proceed, but you must first yield to any vehicles already present in the crossroads

☐ You must temporarily stop and cede before proceeding

Question 16 - Signs and Situations

Car B enters an intersection intending to turn right on a red light, while Car A has a green light and wants to proceed straight through the intersection. Which statement is accurate?

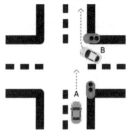

☐ Car A should yield to Car B

☐ Car A must accelerate to pass Car B

☐ Car B should stop and allow Car A to pass

☐ None of these options are correct

Question 17 - Signs and Situations

Before turning left into a driveway, to whom must you yield?

☐   Approaching vehicles

☐   Pedestrians

☐   Both pedestrians and oncoming vehicles

☐   No one (you have the right-of-way)

Question 18 - Signs and Situations

You're following a school bus when its yellow lights begin to flash. What does this indicate?

☐   The bus is signaling for you to pass safely

☐   The bus is preparing to stop for passengers; slow down and be ready to stop

☐   The bus is about to pull over, allowing you to continue at your normal speed

☐   The bus is stopping for passengers; you must stop immediately

Question 19 - Signs and Situations

You approach an intersection with a STOP sign. Where are you required to stop?

☐   Before entering the intersection

☐   In front of the stop line

☐   Prior to the crosswalk

☐   All of the above options apply

Question 20 - Signs and Situations

You arrive at a crossroads wanting to turn left with a green light. Can you proceed?

- ☐ Sure, but only if a Left Turn Permitted sign is present
- ☐ Sure, but first yield to pedestrians and oncoming traffic
- ☐ No, you may only turn left on a green arrow
- ☐ Sure, this is a "protected" turn, and you have the right-of-way

Question 21 - Signs and Situations

You have parked uphill next to a curb. In which direction should you point your front wheels?

- ☐ Away from the curb
- ☐ In any direction
- ☐ Towards the curb
- ☐ Straight

Question 22 - Signs and Situations

You are driving in the right lane of a four-lane highway and see a stopped emergency vehicle with its lights flashing ahead. What should you do?

- ☐ Stop in a non-adjacent lane
- ☐ Move to a non-adjacent lane if possible; otherwise, slow down
- ☐ Proceed carefully
- ☐ Stop immediately

Question 23 - Signs and Situations

The driver is using a hand signal. He/She intends to:

☐ Turn left

☐ Stop

☐ Turn right

☐ Accelerate

Question 24 - Signs and Situations

You notice an emergency vehicle approaching with its flashing lights on. What should you do?

☐ Pull over and stop, regardless of the direction the emergency vehicle is traveling

☐ Continue your journey

☐ Pull over and stop only if the emergency vehicle is traveling in your same direction

☐ Pull over and stop only if the emergency vehicle is traveling in your opposite direction

Question 25 - Signs and Situations

You are about to make a turn at an intersection, and you don't see any other vehicles nearby. Are you still required to signal?

☐ Yes, signal for at least 500 feet.

☐ Yes, signal for at least 300 feet.

☐ Never

☐ Yes, signal for at least 100 feet

FINES & LIMITS

This particular segment is tailored to the laws of your State, featuring 10 questions focused on Fines and Limits. It is known to be one of the most challenging sections, often being the stumbling block for many test-takers.

Total Questions: 10
Correct Answer to pass: 8

Question 1 - Fines & Limits

What is the most common traffic offense for young drivers in California?

- ☐ Speeding
- ☐ Failure to yield vehicles
- ☐ Driving under the influence (DUI)

Question 2 - Fines & Limits

If a California driver under the age of 21 is guilty of transporting alcoholic drinks, the state of California may impound the driver's vehicle for up to _____ days.

- ☐ 60
- ☐ 45
- ☐ 30

Question 3 - Fines & Limits

A California driver under the age of 21 who is found to have a BAC of 0.01% or greater will have his or her license suspended for _____.

- ☐ 90 days
- ☐ 1 year
- ☐ 3 months

Question 4 - Fines & Limits

If you are found guilty of driving without a seat belt for the first time, you will be fined up to _____.

- ☐ $20
- ☐ $50
- ☐ $150

Question 5 - Fines & Limits

If you are convicted of reckless driving that caused someone to be injured, you may _____.

- ☐ be put to jail and/or pay a heavy fine
- ☐ attend an interview at the DMV
- ☐ lose your license for the rest of your life

Question 6 - Fines & Limits

Littering is punishable by a fine of _____ in California. You might also be asked to _____.

- ☐ $1,000; pick up litter
- ☐ $500; pick up litter
- ☐ $50; spend 3 days in jail

Question 7 - Fines & Limits

You will be fined up to _____ if you are convicted of DUI for the first time.

- ☐ $1,500
- ☐ $1,000
- ☐ $2,000

Question 8 - Fines & Limits

In California, your vehicle liability insurance policy must include at least _____ in bodily injury or death coverage for two or more people in any one accident.

- ☐ $50,000
- ☐ $25,000
- ☐ $30,000

Question 9 - Fines & Limits

Your traffic convictions and collisions stay on your record for _____, or longer, depending on the type of conviction.

- ☐ 24 months
- ☐ 36 months
- ☐ 12 months

Question 10 - Fines & Limits

All drivers in California are required by the California Compulsory Financial Responsibility Law to have _____.

- ☐ a vehicle insurance policy
- ☐ proof of financial responsibility
- ☐ a job

DISTRACTED DRIVING TEST

This section is of paramount importance. It will probe your understandIng of contemporary driving distractions, along with the implications of driving under the influence of drugs and medication.

Total Questions: 20
Correct Answer to pass: 16

Question 1 - Distracted Driving

Which of the following statements about cell phones is accurate?

- ☐ It is quicker to make a call while driving
- ☐ The use of a hands-free cell phone while driving is permitted for adults
- ☐ Cell phones can be used while driving for adults
- ☐ If you get a call while you're driving, you should slow down before answering

Question 2 - Distracted Driving

Something happening in the backseat requires your attention while you are driving. What should you do?

- ☐ As you continue to drive, slow down and handle the issue
- ☐ Turn around and cope with the situation, occasionally looking ahead
- ☐ Before addressing the issue, pull over to the side of the road and park your vehicle
- ☐ You should adjust the rearview mirror to see the back seat

Question 3 - Distracted Driving

What should you do before driving if you feel sleepy?

- ☐ Sleep
- ☐ Music-listening
- ☐ consume coffee
- ☐ Exercise

Question 4 - Distracted Driving

What medications, excluding alcohol, can impair one's capacity for safe driving?

- ☐ Prescription drugs
- ☐ Non-prescription medications
- ☐ Medications used to treat migraines, colds, hay fever, various allergies, or to soothe the nerves
- ☐ The entire list above

Question 5 - Distracted Driving

Is it safe to take medications before driving?

- ☐ Only with a valid prescription
- ☐ No
- ☐ Only if the physician states that it won't impair safe driving
- ☐ Only over-the-counter versions

Question 6 - Distracted Driving

It's _____ to text and drive.

☐   legal

☐   legal if you do not exceed 15 mph

☐   legal only when you stop at a STOP sign

☐   illegal

Question 7 - Distracted Driving

Talking on a cell phone while driving increases the likelihood of a collision _____.

☐   up to four times

☐   up to three times

☐   by some more amount

☐   at least twice

Question 8 - Distracted Driving

Is it legal for teenage drivers to talk on their cell phones while driving?

☐   Only when traveling at less than 25 mph

☐   Only if you're on a country road

☐   Yes, as long as you're cautious

☐   It is illegal to use a cell phone while driving

Question 9 - Distracted Driving

To avoid being a distracted driver, you should:

- ☐ smoke, eat, and drink only on straight sections of the road
- ☐ consult maps or use your phone when no other vehicles are around you
- ☐ have all emotionally challenging conversations during your initial hour of driving
- ☐ switch off your cell phone until you arrive at your destination

Question 10 - Distracted Driving

Fatigue can impact your driving by:

- ☐ Compromising your judgement
- ☐ Slowing down your reaction times
- ☐ Reducing your awareness
- ☐ All of the above

Question 11 - Distracted Driving

Potential distractions while driving include:

- ☐ Constantly checking mirrors
- ☐ Checking blind spots
- ☐ Frequently checking the traffic behind you
- ☐ Text messaging and talking on the phone

Question 12 - Distracted Driving

Which types of drugs can influence your ability to safely operate a vehicle?

☐ Over-the-counter drugs

☐ Prescription drugs

☐ Illegal drugs

☐ All of the above mentioned

Question 13 - Distracted Driving

To combat highway hypnosis, drowsiness, and fatigue, drivers should _____ to stay awake while driving.

☐ Take stimulants

☐ Do exercise their eyes

☐ Text message their loved ones

☐ Talk on a cell phone

Question 14 - Distracted Driving

Which of the following activities will not negatively affect your driving on the road?

☐ Eating

☐ Smoking

☐ Drinking coffee

☐ Listening to the radio

Question 15 - Distracted Driving

A minor driver receives a phone call on their cell phone. He/she should:

- ☐ not carry a cell phone while driving
- ☐ not answer the call
- ☐ use a hands-free cell phone to answer the call
- ☐ answer the call only in an emergency

Question 16 - Distracted Driving

Which of the following actions will NOT help prevent distracted driving?

- ☐ Preprogramming your favorite radio stations
- ☐ Adjusting all your mirrors before starting
- ☐ Pre-loosening the coffee cup lid
- ☐ Preplanning the route

Question 17 - Distracted Driving

Which of the following actions is NOT a safe driving practice?

- ☐ Texting and operating visual screen devices while driving
- ☐ Looking forward and sideways while parking
- ☐ Using side mirrors while you drive
- ☐ Humming to music while you drive

Question 18 - Distracted Driving

Be aware of the following potential distractions or impairments while driving:

- ☐   Alcohol, drugs, and certain medications
- ☐   Adjusting electronic controls and vehicle features
- ☐   Listening to loud music, using devices such as cell phones, GPS, and intercoms
- ☐   All of the above mentioned

Question 19 - Distracted Driving

Which statement is accurate?

- ☐   Sending and reading short texts while driving is acceptable
- ☐   If you are lost, you can quickly input navigation instructions while driving
- ☐   Having lunch while driving is safe and time-efficient
- ☐   It is legal to use audio navigation while driving

Question 20 - Distracted Driving

Is it safe to hold something in your lap while driving?

- ☐   Yes, as long as it's not a human or a pet
- ☐   Yes, if it's a small animal
- ☐   Yes, as long as you don't get distracted
- ☐   No way, Never

DRINKING AND DRIVING TEST

This segment delves into the repercussions of driving under the influence of alcohol. It's essential to grasp the restrictions associated with alcohol consumption and its impact on your physical condition while driving.

Total Questions: 20
Correct Answer to pass: 16

Question 1 - Drinking and Driving

What can lead to the suspension of your driving privilege?

- ☐ Having an unopened, sealed container of alcohol in your vehicle
- ☐ Declining to choose a designated sober driver
- ☐ Carrying closed containers of alcohol while working for someone with an off-site liquor sales license
- ☐ Refusing to take a blood and/or urine test

Question 2 - Drinking and Driving

What can help an intoxicated person sober up?

- ☐ Time
- ☐ A cup of coffee
- ☐ Cold and fresh air
- ☐ All of the above

Question 3 - Drinking and Driving

What are the potential penalties for being convicted of driving under the influence of alcohol or drugs?

☐ License suspension

☐ Substantial fines and higher insurance rates

☐ Community service

☐ Any or all of the above

Question 4 - Drinking and Driving

Which is NOT a consequence of consuming alcohol?

☐ Increased alertness

☐ Slow reactions

☐ Impaired judgment

☐ Hindered vision

Question 5 - Drinking and Driving

Which of the following beverages has a standard 1.5-ounce amount of alcohol?

☐ A 5-ounce glass of wine

☐ One can of beer

☐ One shot of 80-proof liquor

☐ Each of the above

Question 6 - Drinking and Driving

Why is consuming alcohol and driving at night particularly dangerous?

- ☐ Alcohol impairs judgment more at night
- ☐ There's a higher chance of encountering drunk drivers
- ☐ Vision is already restricted
- ☐ Roads are busier at night

Question 7 - Drinking and Driving

Which factor does not impact blood alcohol concentration?

- ☐ Time during which alcohol was consumed
- ☐ Body weight
- ☐ Time since the last drink
- ☐ Alcohol type

Question 8 - Drinking and Driving

How does alcohol consumption impact driving ability?

- ☐ Reduces driving skills
- ☐ Negatively affects depth perception
- ☐ Slows down reflexes
- ☐ All of the above

Question 9 - Drinking and Driving

Which of the following actions will result in the mandatory suspension of a minor's license?

☐   Driving when impaired by drugs

☐   Transporting an open beer container

☐   Transporting an open liquor container

☐   Any or all of the preceding

Question 10 - Drinking and Driving

What is the leading cause of death for Americans aged 16 to 24?

☐   Kidney problems

☐   Drunk driving

☐   Drug overdose

☐   Cancer

Question 11 - Drinking and Driving

It is prohibited to have open containers of alcohol in a vehicle in which of the following places?

☐   The driver's seat

☐   The console

☐   beneath the seat

☐   In all of the preceding

Question 12 - Drinking and Driving

Alcohol can have an impact on your:

- ☐ Reaction time
- ☐ Judgment
- ☐ Concentration
- ☐ All of the answers given above are correct.

Question 13 - Drinking and Driving

Drinking and driving can _____.

- ☐ Impair your reflexes
- ☐ Reduce physical control over a vehicle
- ☐ Decrease a driver's awareness of road hazards
- ☐ All of the above

Question 14 - Drinking and Driving

Which of the following statements about drivers under the age of twenty-one is correct?

- ☐ They are not permitted to purchase, drink, or possess alcohol
- ☐ They are permitted to consume limited amounts of alcohol, but not while driving
- ☐ They can buy alcohol but not consume it. They can have trace levels of alcohol in their blood while driving
- ☐ They are allowed to have trace amounts of alcohol in their blood while driving

Question 15 - Drinking and Driving

After consuming a significant amount of alcohol, you can ensure you will not be driving under the influence by:

- ☐ Waiting a day or two
- ☐ Drinking only beer or wine, not hard liquor
- ☐ Waiting at least an hour
- ☐ Waiting at least 30 minutes

Question 16 - Drinking and Driving

Which of the following regions does NOT allow open containers of alcohol?

- ☐ Passenger areas of standard passenger cars
- ☐ Limousine passenger compartments
- ☐ In a passenger car's trunk
- ☐ Motorhome residential areas

Question 17 - Drinking and Driving

Which of the following is not an acceptable substitute for drinking and driving?

- ☐ Public transportation
- ☐ A designated driver
- ☐ A taxi
- ☐ Any of the preceding

Question 18 - Drinking and Driving

A driver who has consumed alcohol is more likely to _____.

- ☐ fail to dim headlights for oncoming traffic
- ☐ drive too fast or too slowly
- ☐ change lanes frequently
- ☐ do all of the preceding tasks

Question 19 - Drinking and Driving

Which of the following activities is illegal for minors?

- ☐ Attempting to buy alcohol
- ☐ Having a blood alcohol concentration (BAC) of 0.02% or higher
- ☐ Alcohol consumption
- ☐ All of the preceding

Question 20 - Drinking and Driving

As a driver's blood alcohol concentration (BAC) increases, which of the following occurs?

- ☐ Alcohol impairs coordination and muscle control
- ☐ Alcohol has a growing impact on the brain of the drinker
- ☐ The first processes to be impacted are self-control and judgment
- ☐ All of the aforementioned

EXAM TEST PRACTICE

Here is the final part of this book. Sit back, relax, and focus. This practice test has the same number of questions as your official DMV exam.

Total Questions: 46
Correct Answer to pass: 38

Question 1 - Mock Exam

If it seems like your tires are losing grip with the road surface, what should you do?

☐ Slow down by easing off the gas pedal

☐ Hold the steering wheel steady

☐ Both actions mentioned above should be taken

Question 2 - Mock Exam

What should a driver overtaking a large truck or commercial vehicle keep an eye out for?

☐ The truck's weight

☐ The truck's No-Zones, including front, rear, and side blind spots

☐ The truck's large mirrors

Question 3 - Mock Exam

On a road with three or more lanes traveling in the same direction, what is the leftmost lane used for?

☐ Passing slower vehicles

☐ Big trucks

☐ Passing faster vehicles

Question 4 - Mock Exam

In which locations is making a U-turn illegal?

- ☐   On a divided highway
- ☐   At a railroad crossing
- ☐   Both of the above

Question 5 - Mock Exam

What should you do if a driver behind you repeatedly flashes their headlights?

- ☐   Move out of the way
- ☐   Switch your headlights to low beam
- ☐   Switch your headlights to high beam

Question 6 - Mock Exam

If you're driving on a single-lane or two-lane road and approach an intersection with a divided highway or a road with three or more lanes, what must you do?

- ☐   Yield the right-of-way to the traffic on the main road
- ☐   Turn left to merge with traffic
- ☐   Stop and turn right to merge with traffic

Question 7 - Mock Exam

Under what circumstances are you allowed to drive to the left of two solid yellow lines in California?

- ☐   Never
- ☐   When overtaking another vehicle
- ☐   When you're in a carpool/High Occupancy Vehicle (HOV) lane that has a left-side entrance

Question 8 - Mock Exam

Where are you allowed to make a U-turn in California?

- ☐ In front of a fire station
- ☐ At a railroad crossing
- ☐ In a residential district

Question 9 - Mock Exam

What should you do to prevent skidding before entering a curve?

- ☐ Slow down by applying the brakes
- ☐ Speed up by pressing the gas pedal
- ☐ Shift to a lower gear

Question 10 - Mock Exam

If there's a vehicle going in the same direction as you, can you cross the double solid yellow lines to overtake it on the left?

- ☐ Yes, if it can be done safely
- ☐ No, overtaking is not allowed here
- ☐ Yes, if there are no vehicles coming from the opposite direction

Question 11 - Mock Exam

When driving at a slower speed than the flow of traffic, you should _____.

- ☐ stick to the lane farthest from the road's shoulder
- ☐ remain in the lane closest to the road's left side
- ☐ stay in the lane closest to the road's right side

Question 12 - Mock Exam

When is double parking permitted?

☐　　Only during a brief stop

☐　　Never

☐　　Only if an individual remains in the vehicle

Question 13 - Mock Exam

"NEV Use Only" lanes are designated for vehicles that _____.

☐　　are allowed to travel faster than the rest of the traffic

☐　　are exclusively for carpooling

☐　　are slow-moving and restricted for neighborhood use

Question 14 - Mock Exam

How should your vehicle's tires be positioned when parked on a level street?

☐　　Parallel to the curb

☐　　Directed towards the curb

☐　　Directed away from the curb

Question 15 - Mock Exam

In which of the following scenarios is it appropriate to honk your horn?

☐　　To urge other drivers to speed up

☐　　To establish eye contact with another driver

☐　　To signal to another driver that they have made a mistake while driving

Question 16 - Mock Exam

Which of the following is accurate about driving when you're upset or angry?

☐ Continue driving; you will eventually calm down

☐ Avoid driving when you're angry or upset

☐ Driving at high speeds will help you calm down

Question 17 - Mock Exam

When you approach an intersection, you should initially look _____ because _____.

☐ left; vehicles approaching from the left have the right-of-way

☐ right; vehicles coming from the right are nearer to you

☐ left; vehicles coming from the left are nearer to you

Question 18 - Mock Exam

When preparing to leave the freeway, you should signal at least ____ seconds before reaching the exit.

☐ 8

☐ 2

☐ 5

Question 19 - Mock Exam

If you have to cross multiple lanes on the freeway, you should _____.

☐ cross two lanes at once if there is room

☐ cross several lanes at once

☐ cross them one lane at a time

Question 20 - Mock Exam

In California, when is it permissible to drive on the shoulder of a road?

- ☐ When you are passing other vehicles
- ☐ When you are moving faster than other traffic
- ☐ Never

Question 21 - Mock Exam

While children are outside, the speed limit is 25 mph within _____ feet of a school.

- ☐ 500–1000
- ☐ 200–500
- ☐ 300–600

Question 22 - Mock Exam

Is it permissible to stop next to a white curb?

- ☐ Yes, but only if you possess a disabled persons' placard or license plate
- ☐ Yes, but just long enough to load or unload passengers or freight
- ☐ Yes, but merely to pick up or drop off passengers or mail

Question 23 - Mock Exam

What should you do when preparing to make a turn?

- ☐ Honk your horn
- ☐ Begin signaling well in advance of the turn
- ☐ Keep your foot resting on the brake pedal

Question 24 - Mock Exam

What else must you do when weather conditions necessitate using your windshield wipers?

☐ Drive in a lower gear

☐ Extend the use of turn signals over a longer distance

☐ Switch on your headlights

Question 25 - Mock Exam

Because of their large size, tractor-trailers often seem to be moving at what speed?

☐ Faster

☐ Backward

☐ Slower

Question 26 - Mock Exam

How far can you drive in a center left-turn lane?

☐ 200 feet

☐ 500 feet

☐ 300 feet

Question 27 - Mock Exam

When is it legal in California to make a left turn against a red light?

☐ Only during times indicated by signs

☐ When transitioning from a one-lane road to a two-lane road

☐ When moving from a one-way street onto another one-way street

Question 28 - Mock Exam

Why should you always check over your shoulder for motorcycles before changing lanes?

- ☐   Motorcycles often have reckless riders

- ☐   They can be difficult to spot

- ☐   Motorcycles are known to change speeds rapidly

Question 29 - Mock Exam

Is it legal to make a U-turn on an undivided roadway in a business district?

- ☐   Yes

- ☐   Yes, but only at intersections

- ☐   Never

Question 30 - Mock Exam

When passing a bicyclist on a two-lane road, how much space must you leave between your vehicle and the bicycle?

- ☐   5 feet

- ☐   3 feet

- ☐   15 feet

Question 31 - Mock Exam

Which statement regarding scanning the road ahead is incorrect?

- ☐   Always keep your eyes fixed on the vehicle in front of you

- ☐   To identify potential hazards early, look well ahead

- ☐   Aim to look about 15 seconds ahead of your vehicle

Question 32 - Mock Exam

In which circumstances should you maintain extra space between your vehicle and the one ahead?

☐ When the driver behind you is trying to pass

☐ When the vehicle in front of you is a large truck

☐ Both scenarios mentioned above

Question 33 - Mock Exam

When is steering with one hand appropriate?

☐ During most turning maneuvers

☐ While backing up

☐ It's never appropriate

Question 34 - Mock Exam

Who has the right-of-way when merging into freeway traffic?

☐ The merging vehicle

☐ The vehicle that's driving the fastest

☐ The traffic already on the freeway

Question 35 - Mock Exam

How should you drive in a work (cone) zone?

☐ Allow additional following distance behind the vehicle in front of you

☐ Reduce your speed

☐ Both of the above

Question 36 - Mock Exam

To prevent sudden maneuvers, how far down the road should you look?

- ☐ 100–200 feet
- ☐ 10–15 seconds
- ☐ 25–100 feet

Question 37 - Mock Exam

If you were parked and are now reentering traffic, _____.

- ☐ honk your horn to gain attention
- ☐ you have the right-of-way
- ☐ the traffic on the road has the right-of-way

Question 38 - Mock Exam

It is illegal to enter an intersection if _____.

- ☐ you are in the right-hand lane
- ☐ you would block other traffic
- ☐ there is a flashing yellow traffic light

Question 39 - Mock Exam

If you are 18 years or older, can you talk on your cell phone while driving?

- ☐ Yes, but only if it's a hands-free phone
- ☐ Never
- ☐ Yes, but only if you are driving on a rural road

Question 40 - Mock Exam

You should never follow within _____ of any emergency vehicle with a siren or flashing lights.

- ☐ 150 feet
- ☐ 300 feet
- ☐ 500 feet

Question 41 - Mock Exam

Are you allowed to pass another vehicle when approaching a curve or a hill?

- ☐ No, never
- ☐ Yes, but only if there is enough space
- ☐ Yes, but you may only pass on the right

Question 42 - Mock Exam

When three lanes are available, which lane provides the smoothest driving?

- ☐ The left lane
- ☐ The middle lane
- ☐ The right lane

Question 43 - Mock Exam

If your vehicle breaks down and you cannot move it completely off the road, where should you stop?

- ☐ Middle of a curb
- ☐ Stop it where your vehicle can be seen from behind
- ☐ Top of a hill

Question 44 - Mock Exam

While driving uphill on a mountain road, you encounter another vehicle that you can't pass. What should you do?

- ☐ Wait for the other vehicle to back up the hill until there is enough room for you to pass
- ☐ Reverse down the hill until you find a place to pull over
- ☐ Call the highway patrol

Question 45 - Mock Exam

You should signal for at least _____, before changing lanes on a freeway.

- ☐ 5 seconds
- ☐ 10 seconds
- ☐ 15 seconds

Question 46 - Mock Exam

You're driving on a highway and notice the vehicle ahead has both right and left turn signals flashing simultaneously. What does this signify?

- ☐ The vehicle ahead has stopped
- ☐ The vehicle ahead is indicating a hazard
- ☐ The vehicle ahead is signaling for you to pass

ANSWER SHEET

PRACTICE TEST 1

Question 1 - Practice Test 1

(B) During a skid, the primary instrument to recover control over the vehicle is the steering wheel. Guide the wheel in the direction the car is skidding. You'll sense when the car is back under your control, at which point you should straighten the wheels.

Question 2 - Practice Test 1

(C) For California drivers under 21, a first-time DUI conviction results in a one-year suspension of driving privileges. Additionally, they will be required to undertake the educational component of a licensed DUI program. Further offenses might require a more extended DUI program, and they won't receive a restricted driver license to attend the DUI program.

Question 3 - Practice Test 1

(B) A continuous yellow line on your side of the road is a sign that overtaking is not allowed in that area.

Question 4 - Practice Test 1

(B) For those under 21, undergoing a handheld breath test is mandatory. Their blood alcohol level should be zero (Zero tolerance rule).

Question 5 - Practice Test 1

(C) At intersections where there are no stop or yield signs, you should yield to pedestrians, vehicles, and bicycles traversing the through road. They have priority.

Question 6 - Practice Test 1

(B) A "speed zone ahead" is a regulatory sign. Upon seeing this sign, you're approaching an area with a reduced speed limit. Start slowing down to ensure you don't exceed the speed limit in that area.

Question 7 - Practice Test 1

(C) In California, the law stipulates that a minor under the age of 18 may not be employed as a paid driver.

Question 8 - Practice Test 1

(C) A California driver with a provisional driver's license who neglects a traffic violation will have his or her license suspended until the driver resolves the violation in court.

Question 9 - Practice Test 1

(B) Warning signs are typically diamond-shaped with black symbols or letters on a yellow background.

Question 10 - Practice Test 1

(B) In California, if an underage driver's preliminary chemical test indicates a BAC of 0.05% or higher, the officer may request a second test. If the second test also shows a BAC of 0.05% or above, the driver can be arrested for DUI, and their license will be suspended.

Question 11 - Practice Test 1

(B) A provisional driver in California who has two instances of being "at fault" in accidents or convictions (or one of each) within a year will be unable to drive solo for a month unless a licensed adult of 25 years or more, or their licensed parent is with them.

Question 12 - Practice Test 1

(A) The total stopping distance is the sum of the distance covered during perception (the distance the vehicle travels from the time a hazard is noticed until the brain comprehends it), reaction (the distance covered from when the brain signals the foot to act until the foot starts to brake), and braking (the distance the vehicle continues to move after the brakes are applied).

Question 13 - Practice Test 1

(B) In California, a parent or a guardian is legally permitted to revoke a minor's driving license.

Question 14 - Practice Test 1

(C) Minors are legally prohibited from using any form of cell phone while driving, including hands-free devices. If the phone rings, they should not answer. This law violation leads to penalties.

Question 15 - Practice Test 1

(B) A provisional driver's license holder in California is prohibited from driving alone between 11:00 p.m. and 5:00 a.m. unless supervised by a qualified adult.

Question 16 - Practice Test 1

(C) A broken yellow line next to a solid yellow line indicates that passing is permitted on the side of the broken line but not on the solid line.

Question 17 - Practice Test 1

(C) If an individual aged between 13 and 20 is convicted for consuming alcohol, their permit or driver's license will be suspended for a year. If they don't have a driver's license yet, the California DMV will delay their eligibility for one.

Question 18 - Practice Test 1

(C) A note, signed and confirmed by a physician, school administrator, or employer, can allow a provisional license holder in California to drive during restricted hours.

Question 19 - Practice Test 1

(C) Unfavorable conditions such as rain, snow, and ice can impair your visibility, thereby extending the distance needed to stop your vehicle safely. During these conditions, you should increase the distance from the vehicle in front of you and apply brakes earlier but more gently than usual.

Question 20 - Practice Test 1

(C) If you are 18 or older and have a California instruction permit, you should always be accompanied by a driver who is at least 18 and has a valid California driver's license. This person should be seated close enough to take control of the vehicle if necessary.

Question 21 - Practice Test 1

(C) Approximately half of California drivers aged between 15 and 19 are found guilty of at least one traffic violation within their first year of operating a vehicle.

Question 22 - Practice Test 1

(C) When you come across a stationary school bus with red lights flashing, you must stop before reaching the bus. Continue to remain stationary until the red lights cease to flash.

Question 23 - Practice Test 1

(B) Gravel or dirt roads do not provide as much traction as roads made of concrete or asphalt. Consequently, stopping takes longer and turning can cause skidding on such roads. Thus, reducing speed is advised.

Question 24 - Practice Test 1

(A) Exit ramps are engineered to enable vehicles to decelerate and exit expressways. Speed limits for the ramp are typically lower.

Question 25 - Practice Test 1

(C) Prior to changing lanes, it's essential to check for traffic both behind and adjacent to your vehicle. Ensure that the lane you intend to switch to is clear of any vehicles.

Question 26 - Practice Test 1

(B) The hand-over-hand steering method can be applied while parking, making low-speed turns, or recovering from a skid. This method begins with your hands positioned at 9 and 3 o'clock or slightly lower at 8 and 4 o'clock. Depending on the direction of the turn, one hand pushes the wheel up while the other releases, reaches across the other arm, grips the wheel, and pulls upwards.

Question 27 - Practice Test 1

(C) As any vehicle makes a turn, its rear wheels follow a path shorter than the front wheels. The longer the vehicle, the larger the difference in the turning path. A large truck might overrun the right curb while trying to make a right turn from the right lane, which explains why large trucks often need to swing wide to successfully make a right turn. When following a large truck, pay attention to its turn signals before attempting to overtake. If the truck seems to be veering left, confirm its turn signals; the driver might actually be planning to turn right but is first swinging wide.

Question 28 - Practice Test 1

(A) An acceleration lane, which lets you increase your speed to match that of the freeway traffic, is usually found at the end of most freeway entrance ramps.

Question 29 - Practice Test 1

(A) Generally, California law prohibits parking in front of any driveway, including your own. However, local jurisdictions in California are allowed to issue permits that enable you to park in front of your own driveway.

Question 30 - Practice Test 1

(A) The driver of a vehicle that is being passed must refrain from increasing speed until the overtaking action is fully completed.

Question 31 - Practice Test 1

(A) Any activity that redirects your attention from the driving task is a distraction. This could include texting or talking on your phone, managing children in the back seat, or lighting a cigarette, among others.

Question 32 - Practice Test 1

(A) When faced with animals or livestock on the road, it's recommended to decelerate and follow the instructions of the person in control of the animals. If a stray animal appears in your way, slow down or stop, assuming it's safe to do so.

Question 33 - Practice Test 1

(A) A crosshatched region (marked by diagonal lines) located adjacent to a disabled parking space is designated as a no parking zone.

Question 34 - Practice Test 1

(A) When hauling anything that extends beyond the fenders on the left side or more than 6 inches beyond the fenders on the right side of a passenger vehicle, you're not allowed to do so. If the cargo extends more than 4 feet from the rear bumper of the vehicle, you must affix a 12-inch red or fluorescent orange square flag or 2 red lights during the night.

Question 35 - Practice Test 1

(B) Light-rail vehicles require significant stopping distances. Always keep a safe distance from these vehicles and never make a turn right in front of an oncoming light-rail vehicle.

Question 36 - Practice Test 1

((A) When approaching an intersection where the traffic lights aren't functioning, you should treat it as a four-way stop. That means you should come to a complete stop before entering the intersection, give way according to the rules for four-way stops, and proceed when it's safe.

Question 37 - Practice Test 1

(C) In California, colored curbs are used to indicate parking rules. A green curb denotes limited time parking as per the posted signs. A yellow curb indicates you can only stop briefly to load or unload passengers or freight. A white curb signals that only passenger pick up and drop off is allowed, but not freight. A red curb means stopping is prohibited for any reason other than obeying another traffic law. Lastly, a blue curb is reserved for individuals with a disabled placard or license plate.

Question 38 - Practice Test 1

(A) According to California law, animals being transported in the back of a pickup truck or other similar vehicle must be securely fastened. This prevents the animal from falling out, jumping, or being ejected from the vehicle.

Question 39 - Practice Test 1

(C) In California, if you are towing a vehicle or trailer, you must stay in the rightmost lane or a lane specifically marked for slower-moving vehicles. If no lanes are marked and there are four or more lanes in your direction, you can only use the two rightmost lanes.

Question 40 - Practice Test 1

(A) While driving behind another vehicle at night, it's crucial to switch your headlights to the low-beam setting. High beams can blind the driver ahead because the light can reflect off the vehicle's rearview mirrors.

PRACTICE TEST 2

Question 1 - Practice Test 2

(B) If your vehicle gets stuck on railroad tracks and a train is coming, avoid trying to free the vehicle. Instead, ensure everyone exits the vehicle and swiftly moves at a 45-degree angle away from the tracks in the direction the train is coming. This way, you and any passengers will not be hit by debris if the car is struck. Contact 911 or call the number displayed on the railroad crossing sign.

Question 2 - Practice Test 2

(B) If you are being tailgated, change lanes if possible, or pull over to let the tailgater go by. Refrain from braking as a warning, as this could worsen an already dangerous situation. Also, do not speed up in an attempt to appease or outrun the tailgater, as some may still follow too closely.

Question 3 - Practice Test 2

(A) When double solid lines are adjacent to your lane, passing or changing lanes is prohibited.

Question 4 - Practice Test 2

(D) When driving on wet pavement at speeds up to 35 mph, modern tires generally disperse water to maintain road contact. However, at higher speeds in deep water, tire channeling becomes less effective, causing the tires to glide on the water like water skis. This phenomenon is called "hydroplaning." At 50 mph or above, hydroplaning can lead to a complete loss of braking and steering control. To avoid hydroplaning, reduce your speed.

Question 5 - Practice Test 2

(A) Warning signs are generally diamond-shaped with black letters or symbols on a yellow background.

Question 6 - Practice Test 2

(C) When the road is covered in snow, you should reduce your speed by half. On wet or icy roads, you should likewise slow down, but by a different amount.

Question 7 - Practice Test 2

(D) If confronted by an aggressive driver, do not provoke them further. Refrain from making eye contact, name-calling, or making rude gestures. For your safety, stay inside your vehicle and continue driving while slowing down and changing lanes to allow the aggressive driver to pass.

Question 8 - Practice Test 2

(D) If you experience a sudden tire blowout, firmly hold the steering wheel and gradually ease off the gas pedal. Apply gentle braking only after regaining control of your vehicle.

Question 9 - Practice Test 2

(D) A solid yellow traffic light serves as a warning that the light will soon turn red. Prepare to stop for a red light, but avoid suddenly stopping if there's a vehicle close behind you to prevent a rear-end collision. If stopping safely isn't possible, cautiously proceed through the intersection.

Question 10 - Practice Test 2

(B) If your rear wheels start to skid, turn the steering wheel in the direction the vehicle is trying to go. Steer left if your rear wheels are sliding left, and steer right if they are sliding right. The rear wheels may overcorrect and begin skidding in the opposite direction; if this happens, turn the steering wheel in that direction as well. This method, known as "steering into the skid," should help regain control of your vehicle.

Question 11 - Practice Test 2

(A) If vehicles approach an intersection from opposite directions at approximately the same time, the vehicle turning left must yield to the vehicle proceeding straight or turning right.

Question 12 - Practice Test 2

(B) Four out of ten collisions are rear-end crashes, primarily caused by tailgating. Ensure at least two seconds elapse between the vehicle in front passing a stationary object and you reaching that same object. In poor or hazardous driving conditions, increase the space cushion to three or even four seconds.

Question 13 - Practice Test 2

(B) Pedestrians and vehicles already in an intersection have the right-of-way. Since a roundabout or rotary is a circular intersection, you must yield the right-of-way to pedestrians and vehicles already in the circle when entering.

Question 14 - Practice Test 2

(B) Two-thirds of deer-vehicle collisions happen in October, November, and December, which is deer breeding season. Exercise caution when driving near deer crossing signs.

Question 15 - Practice Test 2

(B) High beams allow you to see further ahead, but they can create glare by reflecting off fog, rain, or snow, making it harder to see. Use low beams in fog, rain, or snow.

Question 16 - Practice Test 2

(B) You cannot pass a vehicle on the left if your lane has a solid yellow center line. Even with a broken yellow center line, you may not pass on the left if you cannot return to the right lane before reaching a solid yellow line for that lane.

Question 17 - Practice Test 2

(A) Exit ramps allow vehicles to leave expressways. Speed limits are often reduced at exit ramps.

Question 18 - Practice Test 2

(D) If the street is too narrow for a U-turn, make a three-point turn to change your vehicle's direction. This maneuver should only be performed when the street is narrow, visibility is good, traffic is light on both sides, the turn is allowed, and no other option is available.

Question 19 - Practice Test 2

(C) A single standard alcoholic drink (1.5 ounces of liquor, 5 ounces of wine, or 12 ounces of beer) can raise your blood alcohol content (BAC) to 0.02% or higher. At a BAC of 0.02%, your ability to track a moving target visually and perform two tasks simultaneously is impaired.

Question 20 - Practice Test 2

(D) When another vehicle is passing you on the left, reduce your speed slightly and maintain your position in the center of your lane until the vehicle has safely passed and is ahead of you. Once the vehicle has safely passed, you can resume your normal speed.

Question 21 - Practice Test 2

(D) When turning right on a multi-lane road, you should generally use the rightmost lane, unless signs, signals, or lane markings permit turning from multiple lanes.

Question 22 - Practice Test 2

(B) When an emergency vehicle with flashing lights, a siren, or an air horn is approaching you from any direction, you should pull over to the right and stop. However, if you are already in an intersection, proceed through the intersection before stopping.

Question 23 - Practice Test 2

(C) Flashing red lights, lowered crossing gates, or ringing bells at a railroad crossing indicate that a train is approaching or passing. You must stop at least 15 feet from the nearest rail of the tracks and remain stopped until the lights or bells have stopped and the crossing gates are fully raised.

Question 24 - Practice Test 2

(C) You should not pass a vehicle on the right if it is making or about to make a right turn. Ensure the passing lane is clear before attempting to pass.

Question 25 - Practice Test 2

(A) When driving in open country at night, use your high-beam headlights, as they allow you to see much further than low beams.

Question 26 - Practice Test 2

(B) Crosswalks can be either marked or unmarked, and they may be present whether or not there are crosswalk lines.

Question 27 - Practice Test 2

(D) Tractor-trailers often appear to be moving slower than they actually are due to their large size. Maintain a safe distance and be cautious when passing or turning around them.

Question 28 - Practice Test 2

(D) Always look both ways at railroad crossings, crosswalks, and intersections. Be sure to follow the left-right-left rule to check for approaching pedestrians, vehicles, or trains.

Question 29 - Practice Test 2

(A) You should always signal before passing another vehicle to ensure safe and clear communication with other drivers on the road.

Question 30 - Practice Test 2

(A) Your horn should be used to warn pedestrians or other drivers of potential danger. However, avoid using your horn unnecessarily or to express anger at others, as this can be a sign of aggressive driving.

Question 31 - Practice Test 2

(D) The type of alcohol does not affect your BAC, as the amount of ethanol matters rather than the form it takes. All alcoholic drinks contain different amounts of ethanol, but 1.5 ounces of 80-proof liquor, 5 ounces of wine, 12 ounces of beer, and 12 ounces of wine cooler have the same amount of ethanol.

Question 32 - Practice Test 2

(C) As the driver, you are responsible for ensuring all children in the vehicle are properly secured. Fines and penalty points may apply for each violation.

Question 33 - Practice Test 2

(C) The appropriate hand signal for a right turn is a left arm bent at 90 degrees, pointing upward.

Question 34 - Practice Test 2

(C) Treat a flashing red light like a stop sign, meaning you must stop before entering the intersection, yield to traffic and pedestrians, and proceed when safe.

Question 35 - Practice Test 2

(A) Bridges, overpasses, and ramps are especially vulnerable to icing because they are exposed to more moisture and cold air. When driving on these surfaces in freezing weather, use caution.

Question 36 - Practice Test 2

(C) Vehicles already on the expressway have the right-of-way when a vehicle is merging.

Question 37 - Practice Test 2

(D) Stopping in the middle of an intersection is illegal, even for approaching emergency vehicles. Instead, continue through the intersection and pull over immediately afterward.

Question 38 - Practice Test 2

(C) At an all-way stop, yield to vehicles that arrived before you. Vehicles should proceed in the order they arrived, with the first vehicle to arrive going first.

Question 39 - Practice Test 2

(C) Blind pedestrians have the absolute right-of-way. Yield to the pedestrian, stopping if necessary. Avoid honking your horn near a blind pedestrian, as it may startle them or mask essential auditory cues.

Question 40 - Practice Test 2

(B) It is likely safe to merge back in front of the vehicle once you can see its entire front bumper in your rear-view mirror.

ROAD SIGNS

Question 1 - Road Signs

(A) The image illustrates that overtaking on the left is permissible when the road ahead is clear. Overtaking and passing should be done with caution due to oncoming traffic.

Question 2 - Road Signs

(D) This sign denotes that a rest area is available on the right.

Question 3 - Road Signs

(C) This warning sign indicates the presence of a playground ahead.

Question 4 - Road Signs

(A) This sign warns drivers that a nearby side road crosses a railroad track. When turning onto the side road, proceed with caution.

Question 5 - Road Signs

(C) This sign denotes that you are not permitted to park in a handicap zone unless you have the necessary permit.

Question 6 - Road Signs

(C) A vehicle with a reflective triangular orange sign on the rear identifies it as a low-speed or slow-moving vehicle, which is typically defined as a motor vehicle with a top speed of no more than 25 mph. Farm vehicles and road maintenance vehicles are examples of these type of slow-moving vehicles. Slow down and proceed with caution if you come across one of these vehicles.

Question 7 - Road Signs

(B) The blue-and-white signs direct you to services such as gas stations, fast food restaurants, motels, and hospitals. Picture B indicates that there is a hospital ahead.

Question 8 - Road Signs

(C) In this case the larger sign alerts you to the impending arrival of a speed zone. The speed limit is indicated by the smaller sign. The speed limit will be reduced to 45 mph ahead in this case. So be prepared to slow down so that you don't go over the speed limit.

Question 9 - Road Signs

(A) Typically, vertical rectangular signs provide instructions or inform you of traffic laws. Drivers, pedestrians, and cyclists are given instructions by such regulatory signs.

Question 10 - Road Signs

(C) This sign denotes that the road ahead curves in the direction indicated by the arrow.

Quesiton 11 - Road Signals Full

(A) This is a warning sign that may be placed ahead of the railroad crossing. Vehicles must slow down, look, listen, and be prepared to stop at the crossing ahead.

Question 12 - Road Signs

(A) The sequential arrow panels can be used in work zones 24 hours a day, seven days a week. This sign indicates that the lane ahead is closed and that you should take the lane to your left.

Question 13 - Road Signs

(C) This sign denotes that the divided highway is ending ahead. The road will be converted to a two-way street. Keep to the right and keep an eye out for oncoming traffic.

Question 14 - Road Signs

(B) This sign is normally displayed at an intersection with a combination of signals, including a green arrow pointing left. When the

green arrow is lit, you may make a protected left turn; oncoming traffic will be stopped at a red light. This sign indicates that if the green arrow disappears and a steady green light appears, you may still make a left turn, but you must now yield to oncoming traffic before turning.

Question 15 - Road Signs

(B) A disabled crossing is indicated by the sign ahead. Slow down and take your time.

Question 16 - Road Signs

(D) This indicates a warning signal. Bicyclists and pedestrians frequently cross the road in the vicinity of the sign. You must drive cautiously and be prepared to stop.

Question 17 - Road Signs

(B) This sign denotes a bicycle crossing. This sign forewarns you that a bikeway will cross the road ahead.

Question 18 - Road Signs

(C) If you see this sign while driving in the left lane, you should turn left at the next intersection.

Question 19 - Road Signs

(D) This warning sign indicates that there will be a double curve ahead. The road ahead bends to the right, then to the left. (A winding road sign would be posted instead if there was a triple curve ahead.) Slow down, stay to the right, and do not pass.

Question 20 - Road Signs

(D) The pedestrian signals are only used to direct pedestrian traffic. This pedestrian signal indicates that pedestrians may enter the crosswalk to cross the road. (Older signals displayed the word "WALK" instead.) A signal with an upraised hand warns pedestrians not to enter the crosswalk. (Older signals displayed the words "DO NOT WALK" instead.)

Question 21 - Road Signs

(A) This navigational sign indicates the presence of a hospital ahead.

Question 22 - Road Signs

(A) This symbol indicates an exit number. This is the number assigned to a highway exit at a junction. If an interchange has more than one exit, a letter may be added to indicate which exit it is: For example: 117A, 117B, and so on.

Question 23 - Road Signs

(A) This is a gas station service sign

Question 24 - Road Signs

(C) This is a speed advisory sign at a roundabout. In the roundabout, the speed limit is 15 mph.

Question 25 - Road Signs

(A) This is a traffic control sign. This sign indicates that traffic must only make a left turn.

Question 26 - Road Signs

(A) The arrow signifies a right turn. In contrast, a red slash inside a red circle symbolizes "no." Turning right is prohibited by this regulatory sign. This sign is typically located on the right side of the road or above a driving lane.

Question 27 - Road Signs

(B) This service sign indicates that a telephone service is available ahead.

Question 28 - Road Signs

(B) This sign is next to a route marker sign. It indicates that you will need to turn right soon to enter or continue on that route.

Question 29 - Road Signs

(B) This sign shows the safest speed to enter or depart an expressway. Reduce your speed to the specified speed (in this case, 30 mph).

Question 30 - Road Signs

(B) A single broken (dashed) yellow line may exist on a two-lane, two-way road. Vehicles on either side may pass if it is safe to do so.

Question 31 - Road Signs

(D) Lane use control signs are rectangular, black-and-white signs that indicate whether or not turning from specific lanes is required at an intersection. You are only permitted to drive in the direction indicated for your traffic lane.

Question 32 - Road Signs

(B) This sign shows the presence of a four-way intersection ahead. Drivers should be alert for cross traffic entering the roadway.

Question 33 - Road Signs

(A) This sign indicates a low-ground clearance railroad crossing. The railroad crossing is elevated enough that a vehicle with a large wheelbase or limited ground clearance could become stranded on the tracks. A car driver should have no trouble navigating this type of railroad crossing unless he or she is towing a trailer or driving a mobile home with low ground clearance.

Question 34 - Road Signs

(B) If your lane has a broken or dashed line (white or yellow), you may pass if it is safe to do so.

Question 35 - Road Signs

(C) A stop sign is an eight-sided white-on-red sign that indicates other traffic has the right-of-way. Always come to a complete stop before proceeding and yield to approaching vehicles.

Question 36 - Road Signs

(D) Work zone signs notify drivers of unusual or potentially hazardous conditions on or around the traveled route. These signs include black lettering or symbols on an orange background. If you encounter these signals, slow down and pay close attention.

Question 37 - Road Signs

(A) The shape of the arrow indicates that you are going to enter a winding road. A winding road has at least three turns. Take your time and slow down.

Question 38 - Road Signs

(C) When the road surface is wet, it becomes slippery. This sign is frequently found near bridges and overpasses.

Question 39 - Road Signs

(B) This is a freeway interchange sign. This sign warns you that you are approaching an interchange.

Question 40 - Road Signs

(D) This sign indicates that you must never park on the left side of the sign.

Question 41 - Road Signs

(B) This sign advises that the road ahead will be divided into two lanes. To separate opposing lanes, a divider, also known as a median, will be used. Continue right.

Question 42 - Road Signs

(B) This sign indicates that you are driving in the wrong way. Turn around.

Question 43 - Road Signs

(D) This sign denotes that the maximum nighttime speed limit is 45 mph.

Question 44 - Road Signs

(A) This is an emergency vehicle warning sign. It indicates the possibility of emergency vehicles from fire stations or other emergency facilities entering the route. If an emergency vehicle approaches from any direction and is sounding a siren, blowing an air horn, or flashing lights, you must surrender to it.

Question 45 - Road Signs

(D) This sign can be located at the end of various T-intersections. It means that before turning right or left onto the through route, you must yield the right of way or come to a complete stop.

Question 46 - Road Signs

(C) This sign indicates that U-turns are not permitted in this area.

Question 47 - Road Signs

(B) This sign indicates a T-junction. This sign indicates that the road you're on is about to come to an end. Prepare to make a right or left turn. Yield to oncoming traffic.

Question 48 - Road Signs

(A) This is an animal crossing sign. In this area, the animal represented on the sign (in this case, a deer) is common. Keep a watch out for animals like this crossing the street, particularly at dawn and night. Deer, elk, and other species roam in herds. Keep an eye out for more if you spot one. A collision with a large animal has the potential to kill the animal, do significant damage to your vehicle, and perhaps injure someone in your vehicle.

Question 49 - Road Signs

(C) This sign warns drivers not to exceed the specified speed limit in a school zone or school crossing when there are children present. In this scenario, the maximum permissible speed is 15 mph.

Question 50 - Road Signs

(B) This sign is indicating a service. It is recommended that drivers use lodging facilities if necessary.

Question 51 - Road Signs

(A) This white diamond sign shows that the road is reserved for high-occupancy vehicles (HOVs) at the times specified from Monday to Friday.

Question 52 - Road Signs

(D) At an intersection, a stop sign accompanied by this sign denotes that the intersection is a four-way

stop. Each approaching road has a stop sign and a "4-Way" sign.

Question 53 - Road Signs

(B) This sign warns you that you are approaching a T-intersection from the terminating roadway. At the T-intersection, you must turn left or right after yielding the right-of-way to through traffic if necessary.

Question 54 - Road Signs

(A) This sign advises you to turn right onto Route 47 and go north.

Question 55 - Road Signs

(B) This is a guide sign indicating that you are approaching an airport.

Question 56 - Road Signs

(A) This sign denotes the presence of a side road ahead. Keep an eye out for oncoming vehicles from that direction.

Question 57 - Road Signs

(B) This sign indicates a sharp left turn. Slow down (in this case, to the recommended speed of 25 mph), keep right as you turn, and do not pass

Question 58 - Road Signs

(D) A speed limit sign specifies the top legal speed allowed on the expressway under ideal driving circumstances.

Question 59 - Road Signs

C) This sign warns of a road closure ahead, yet an alternate route is only 1,000 feet away.

Question 60 - Road Signs

(B) This sign indicates that there will be a bump in the road ahead. To avoid losing control, slow down.

Question 61 - Road Signs

(B) White lines separate traffic lanes traveling in the same direction. You must drive between the lane markings.

Question 62 - Road Signs

(C) This sign indicates that road maintenance is being done. Slow down, exercise caution, and follow all signs and instructions. Move into a lane that is further away from the workers if feasible.

Question 63 - Road Signs

(A) Most warning signs are diamond-shaped with a yellow background. This sign warns you that a stop sign is about to appear. Prepare to come to a complete stop and yield. Before any stop line or crosswalk placed on the pavement, you must come to a complete stop.

Question 64 - Road Signs

(C) This pentagonal (five-sided) sign indicates that you are approaching a school zone and be cautious.

Question 65 - Road Signs

(D) A prohibitory sign with a red circle and slash symbolizes "no." This sign advises that no left turns are allowed in this location.

Question 66 - Road Signs

(B) This sign denotes an exit number. These signs point you in the direction of bike routes, parking lots, mile markers, and specific exits. Enter the milepost number and the exit number to see how far you are from the exit you want to take.

Question 67 - Road Signs

This symbol represents a soft shoulder. The dirt along the road is soft. Never, unless in an emergency, leave the pavement.

Question 68 - Road Signs

(A) This sign indicates that a traffic island or divider is ahead. Maintain your position to the left of this stumbling block.

Question 69 - Road Signs

(A) A red slash inside a red circle means "no." This sign indicates that driving on railroad tracks are prohibited.

Question 70 - Road Signs

(D) A red slash inside a red circle means "no." According to this regulatory sign, pedestrians are not permitted to cross here.

Question 71 - Road Signs

(A) Lanes of traffic moving in the opposing directions are divided by yellow lines. A solid yellow line should only be crossed while turning left.

Question 72 - Road Signs

(D) The presence of a flagger (flag person) is indicated by this work zone sign. Construction zones on highways or streets typically have flaggers present. To safely direct traffic through certain places, they wear orange vests, shirts, or jackets and wave red flags or use STOP/SLOW paddles. Follow the flagger's instructions.

Question 73 - Road Signs

(A) When you see this sign while driving on the main road, be prepared for other cars and trucks to enter your lane.

Question 74 - Road Signs

(A) This is a warning sign noting that a narrow bridge is ahead. Although the bridge has two lanes of traffic, there is very little clearance.

Question 75 - Road Signs

(B) This sort of warning sign notifies drivers in advance of a lane reduction. This sign signals that the right lane is about to stop. Drivers in the right lane must merge to the left. Drivers in the left lane should allow vehicles in the right lane to merge smoothly.

Question 76 - Road Signs

(A) This sign indicates a bicycle lane intended for bicyclists. Normally, cars and trucks should not use this lane. In many (but not all) states, cars, and trucks may travel in this lane for a short distance when ready to turn at the next intersection.

Question 77 - Road Signs

(A) A Y-intersection is represented by this symbol. The road ahead is divided into two halves. If traffic crosses your path, be prepared to turn in either direction.

Question 78 - Road Signs

(D) Guide signs provide information to drivers regarding the sort of route they are on, forthcoming highway entrances and exits, and distances to various destinations. Guide signs in the shape of a shield are often used to indicate US Routes and interstate highways. This sign indicates that you are on Interstate 95 (I-95), which connects Maine and Florida.

Question 79 - Road Signs

(C) The sign features the International Symbol of Access for Disabled People. This means that only those with disability parking permits will be able to use these spaces. To park in these areas, you must get a disability parking placard or disabled license plates from your state.

Question 80 - Road Signs

(B) This sign alerts drivers to the presence of cattle on the route.

Question 81 - Road Signs

(C) In North America, raising one's hand with the thumb expresses a desire to hitch a ride. A red slash inside a red circle means "no." Hitchhiking is illegal on this stretch of road, according to this sign. Please do not stop here to pick up hitchhikers.

Question 82 - Road Signs

(D) This is a route marker sign for the United States. A route marker sign's shape and color identify the type of road you're on. Shield-shaped signs are commonly used to indicate US Routes and interstate routes. This sign shows that you are on US Highway 40. The United States Routes are a network of roads and highways that were built decades before the Interstate Highway System. US Route 40 was built in 1926 and goes from Silver Summit, Utah to Atlantic City, New Jersey.

Question 83 - Road Signs

(C) This symbol indicates that a pedestrian crosswalk is ahead. Drivers must give pedestrians the right of way.

Question 84 - Road Signs

(A) This is a wayfinding sign. This indicates that food is available

Question 85 - Road Signs

(C) If you notice this sign and are traveling slower than the majority of traffic, change to the right lane so that quicker traffic on the left can pass you.

Question 86 - Road Signs

(B) This one-way sign instructs drivers to only proceed in the direction indicated by the arrow.

Question 87 - Road Signs

(D) According to this sign, the main road will bend to the left, with a side road entering from the right. When approaching this crossroads, use additional caution. A car arriving from around the curve who is ready to enter the main road from a side road may not spot you approaching from around the curve and may pull out in front of you.

Question 88 - Road Signs

(D) This sign indicates that traffic may flow on both sides of the road.

Question 89 - Road Signs

(C) The speed restriction is 40 miles per hour, as shown by this sign. In ideal conditions, this is the fastest you can travel.

Question 90 - Road Signs

(C) This sign cautions that a low point on the road is ahead. Slow down for your own peace of mind and control. Proceed with caution and be ready to turn around if the dip becomes flooded.

Question 91 - Road Signs

(B) This sign indicates alternate routes during road closures or construction. Take note of these cues.

Question 92 - Road Signs

(D) A white line separates two lanes traveling in the same direction. To pass or change lanes, you may cross a broken line. If it's a straight line, you should normally stay in your lane.

Question 93 - Road Signs

(D) This sign regulates traffic and instructs drivers whether to turn left or straight.

Question 94 - Road Signs

(C) A red slash inside a red circle means "no." The wording on this regulatory sign is "No Parking." Parking is not allowed at this sign.

Question 95 - Road Signs

(B) This sign instructs you to proceed straight. You can't turn around here.

Question 96 - Road Signs

(C) The center lane is for left turns (or U-turns when allowed) and can be utilized by vehicles traveling in either direction. On the pavement, left-turn arrows for one-way traffic alternate with left-turn arrows for the opposite direction. These lanes are denoted by solid and broken (dashed) yellow lines on each side.

Question 97 - Road Signs

(B) A yield sign is the only form of sign with a downward-pointing triangle shape. Before proceeding, you must slow down and yield to oncoming traffic and pedestrians when you come to a yield sign. Be prepared to make a stop for them as well.

Question 98 - Road Signs

(B) This unusual lane control sign informs that all vehicles in this lane must make a U-turn. This sign may be accompanied by a traffic signal, with illuminated U-turn arrows showing when vehicles can do U-turns.

Question 99 - Road Signs

(B) Mileposts are spaced at regular intervals to keep drivers aware of them. They are placed along the road's edge to convey information to drivers about their location on the roadway for navigation and emergency purposes. The number on the milepost usually indicates the distance in miles to the state line or the end of the road.

Question 100 - Road Signs

(B) The majority of public crossings have crossbuck signs and railroad flashing light signals. The same rules that apply to YIELD signs apply to these signs as well.

SIGNS AND SITUATIONS

Question 1 - Signs and Situations

(D) Lane use control signals are special overhead signals that indicate which lanes of a roadway may be utilized in various directions at different times. A flashing yellow "X" denotes that this lane is solely for left turns.

Question 2 - Signs and Situations

(D) Vehicles moving in either direction must stop at least 20 feet from a school bus that has stopped with its red lights flashing. They must remain stopped until the bus starts its motion or until the bus driver or a traffic police waves them on.

Question 3 - Signs and Situations

(D) This is a reserved lane. This lane is restricted to specific types of vehicles. High-occupancy vehicle (HOV) lanes and bus lanes are two examples. Keep an eye out for signs stating which cars are permitted to use the lane.

Question 4 - Signs and Situations

(C) When two vehicles approach an intersection at roughly the same moment, the vehicle on the left must yield to the one on the right. In the absence of this rule, the vehicle turning left must yield to approaching traffic. Car A must yield to Car B in this situation.

Question 5 - Signs and Situations

(A) If your brakes fail while driving downhill, the vehicle may begin to roll forward. You can configure the transmission to counteract this movement. Set your manual transmission to Reverse. Set the automatic transmission to Park if you have one.

Question 6 - Signs and Situations

(C) At an uncontrolled intersection, a vehicle must yield to pedestrians in a marked or unmarked crosswalk. After considering pedestrians, each vehicle must yield to the one on its right. Consequently, Vehicle C must yield to Vehicle B, and Vehicle A must yield to Vehicle C.

Question 7 - Signs and Situations

(B) When passing a stopped emergency vehicle, you must slow down. If possible, also change to a non-adjacent lane, leaving at least one empty lane between you and the emergency vehicle.

Question 8 - Signs and Situations

(C) If your vehicle's brakes fail while parked uphill, it may start rolling backward. To counter this movement, set your transmission accordingly. For manual transmissions, set it to first gear for maximum forward torque. For automatic transmissions, set it to Park.

Question 9 - Signs and Situations

(B) Always follow directions from a police officer, even if it means disregarding other traffic devices or rules. For example, drive through a red light or stop sign if a police officer waves you through.

Question 10 - Signs and Situations

(B) Consider a flashing red signal to be a STOP sign. That is, you must come to a complete stop before crossing the intersection, yield to oncoming vehicles and pedestrians, and then proceed cautiously when it is safe to do so.

Question 11 - Signs and Situations

(A) When railroad crossing signals indicate an approaching train, stop at least 15 feet from the nearest rail. Trains are at least six feet wider than the tracks they run on, so maintain a safe distance. Even after the train passes, signals may continue to flash or sound and the gate may stay lowered, indicating a second train is approaching.

Question 12 - Signs and Situations

(A) You must come to a complete stop and yield to all traffic and pedestrians ahead. You can then proceed when the intersection is clear and there are no vehicles approaching that may present a hazard.

Question 13 - Signs and Situations

(A) High-occupancy vehicle (HOV) lanes are designed for vehicles with multiple occupants. This sign means that this lane is an HOV 2+ lane, which requires at least two occupants in each vehicle. In other words, a driver and at least one passenger. An HOV 3+ lane would require a driver and at least two passengers.

Question 14 - Signs and Situations

(A) When two vehicles arrive at an uncontrolled intersection about the same time, the vehicle on the left must yield. Car A must yield in this situation.

Question 15 - Signs and Situations

(C) After yielding to all pedestrians and vehicles already in the junction, you can proceed on a green signal.

Question 16 - Signs and Situations

(A) If you have a green light, you may continue through the intersection, but you must first yield to all pedestrians and vehicles already in the intersection. In this case, Car A must yield to Car B since Car B has already entered the intersection.

Question 17 - Signs and Situations

(C) Prior to making a left turn off the road, you must yield to all pedestrians and oncoming traffic.

Question 18 - Signs and Situations

(B) When a school bus driver activates the flashing yellow lights just before stopping for passengers, you should slow down and prepare to stop. Once the school bus's red lights start flashing, you must stop at least 20 feet away from the bus.

Question 19 - Signs and Situations

(D) At a STOP sign, you must stop before the stop line. If there isn't a stop line, stop before the crosswalk. If there isn't a crosswalk either, stop before entering the intersection.

Question 20 - Signs and Situations

(B) You may turn left on a green light after yielding to pedestrians, oncoming vehicles, and vehicles already in the intersection.

Question 21 - Signs and Situations

(A) When parking uphill parallel to a curb, point your wheels away from the curb and allow your vehicle to roll back slightly so the rear part of the front wheel on the curb side rests against the curb. If your brakes fail, the curb will prevent your car from rolling backward. Ensure you still engage your parking brake and leave your car in the appropriate gear.

Question 22 - Signs and Situations

(B) Upon encountering a stopped emergency vehicle, sanitation vehicle, utility vehicle, or tow truck with flashing lights, move to a non-adjacent lane if possible, leaving at least one vacant lane between your vehicle and the stopped vehicle. If this isn't possible or is unsafe, slow down as you pass the vehicle.

Question 23 - Signs and Situations

(A) The driver intends to turn left.

Question 24 - Signs and Situations

(A) When an emergency vehicle approaches you from either direction with its siren and flashing lights activated, you must clear any intersection, yield to the emergency vehicle, pull over to the nearest edge of the road, and remain stopped until the emergency vehicle has passed.

Question 25 - Signs and Situations

(D) You must signal for at least 100 feet before making a turn. Even if no other vehicles are visible, you must still signal. The most dangerous vehicle could be the one you don't see.

FINE & LIMITS

Question 1 - Fines & Limits

(A) In California, speeding accounts for over half of all teen traffic convictions.

Question 2 - Fines & Limits

(C) If you are under the age of 21 and are convicted of having alcoholic beverages in your vehicle, the court may suspend your license for a year and punish you up to $1,000. Your vehicle may potentially be impounded for up to 30 days by the state of California.

Question 3 - Fines & Limits

(B) A California driver under the age of 21 who is found to have a BAC of 0.01% or more will have his or her driving privileges banned for one year. (A single alcoholic drink will result in a BAC of more than 0.01% for the average person.)

Question 4 - Fines & Limits

(A) If you are found guilty of driving without a seat belt in California, you will be penalized up to $20 for the first offense and up to $50 for each subsequent infraction.

Question 5 - Fines & Limits

(A) If you are convicted of careless driving that causes injury to another person in California, you will be fined, sentenced to jail, or both.

Question 6 - Fines & Limits

(A) If you are convicted of littering, you will have to pay a $1,000 fine. You may also be expected to pick up litter.

Question 7 - Fines & Limits

(B) If you are convicted of DUI for the first time, you will be fined between $390 and $1,000, sentenced to jail for up to six months, your driver license will be banned for at least six months, and your vehicle may be seized.

Question 8 - Fines & Limits

(C) In California, your vehicle's liability insurance policy must provide at least $30,000 in bodily injury or death coverage for two or more people in any one accident.

Question 9 - Fines & Limits

(B) Convictions for traffic violations and crashes are recorded on your record for 36 months or longer, depending on the type of conviction.

Question 10 - Fines & Limits

(B) All California drivers are required to maintain financial responsibility (liability coverage) at all times under the Compulsory Financial Responsibility Law. Most drivers prefer to obtain a vehicle insurance coverage to meet this need. However, there are three other options for staying financially responsible: Deposit $35,000 with the DMV, secure a $35,000 surety bond, or obtain a self-insurance certificate from the DMV.

DISTRACTED DRIVING

Question 1 - Distracted Driving

(B) It is preferable to use a hands-free or speaker phone while driving if you are an adult driver and absolutely must use your phone. In several states, it is illegal and not advised to use a mobile phone while driving.

Question 2 - Distracted Driving

(C) Never turn around to attend to the needs of passengers, kids, or animals while you are driving. Pull over to the side of the road and park your vehicle if you need to attend to any passengers or animals.

Question 3 - Distracted Driving

(A) Although stimulants, physical activity, and music can help you stay alert, sleeping is the greatest cure for fatigue. Consult a doctor if, despite receiving 9 hours of sleep, you still feel exhausted.

Question 4 - Distracted Driving

(D) Before taking a medication, look for any warnings about its effect(s) while you are driving. Ask your doctor or pharmacist about any potential side effects if you are unsure if it is safe to take the medication and drive. Drugs used to treat headaches, colds, hay fever or other allergies, or to calm nerves might cause drowsiness and have an impact on a person's ability to drive. Similar to how alcohol does, some prescription medications can impair your reflexes, judgment, eyesight, and awareness.

Question 5 - Distracted Driving

(C) Many over-the-counter and prescription drugs might make you sleepy. Only use drugs while driving if your doctor says they won't impair your ability to drive safely.

Question 6 - Distracted Driving

(D) Texting while driving currently accounts for 25% of all car accidents in the US and is the greatest cause of death for youths. Texting while driving is illegal.

Question 7 - Distracted Driving

(A) Talking on a cell phone while driving increases your chances of being in a crash by up to four times. This is because the talk is taking your focus away from driving. Sending text messages (texting) while driving increases your chances of being in an accident by up to eightfold.

Question 8 - Distracted Driving

(D) Cell phones are not permitted to be used by underage drivers while driving, unless to notify an emergency.

Question 9 - Distracted Driving

(D) Distractions, even on straight roads or empty roads, should be avoided. Refrain from eating, drinking, smoking, texting, reading, or engaging in difficult conversations while driving. If possible, turn off your phone and keep it off until you have completed driving for the day.

Question 10 - Distracted Driving

(D) Fatigue can impair your judgement, slow down your reaction times, and decrease your awareness of your surroundings.

Question 11 - Distracted Driving

(D) Distractions while driving include text messaging, talking on the phone, dealing with children, and lighting a cigarette, among other activities that draw your attention away from the road.

Question 12 - Distracted Driving

(D) Over-the-counter drugs, prescription drugs, and illegal drugs can all impact your ability to drive safely.

Question 13 - Distracted Driving

(B) Highway hypnosis or drowsiness while driving can result from monotonous road and traffic conditions, the hum of wind, tires, and the engine. Drivers can avoid highway hypnosis by continuously moving their eyes and monitoring traffic and road signs around them.

Question 14 - Distracted Driving

(D) Activities that require the use of your hands should be avoided while driving. Listening to the radio, however, can help you stay alert.

Question 15 - Distracted Driving

(B) It is against the law for minors to use a cell phone while driving. If a cell phone rings, they should not answer the call. Violators of this law may face fines.

Question 16 - Distracted Driving

(C) You should set up your cab before starting your trip, but eating and drinking should be done at rest stops.

Question 17 - Distracted Driving

(A) Driving while operating a visual screen device or texting is illegal and prohibited by law.

Question 18 - Distracted Driving

(D) You should also be aware of potential distractions and impairments, as they can affect your driving abilities. All the listed factors, including emotional and physical states like fatigue, anger, illness, stress, and fear, can impair your driving skills.

Question 19 - Distracted Driving

(D) Texting or eating while driving increases the risk of an accident. If you are lost, pull over and input navigation instructions. However, using audio navigation while driving is permitted.

Question 20 - Distracted Driving

(D) It is dangerous to engage in any activity that takes your eyes off the road while driving, such as removing clothing, applying makeup, reading, eating, or drinking. Avoid holding a person, pet, or package in your lap or arms.

DRINKING AND DRIVING

Question 1 - Drinking and Driving

(D) Refusing to undergo mandatory blood and/or urine tests may result in the suspension of your driving privilege.

Question 2 - Drinking and Driving

(A) Only time can effectively eliminate alcohol from a person's system. Coffee and fresh air might alleviate some symptoms of intoxication but will not reduce the actual level of impairment.

Question 3 - Drinking and Driving

(D) Upon conviction of driving under the influence of alcohol or drugs, penalties may include license suspension, significant fines, and community service.

Question 4 - Drinking and Driving

(A) Alcohol consumption impairs vision, slows reactions, and affects judgment but does not increase alertness.

Question 5 - Drinking and Driving

(D) A standard serving of alcohol is typically 1.5 ounces, regardless of the type of drink.

Question 6 - Drinking and Driving

(C) Drinking alcohol and driving at night is especially risky because vision is already restricted due to darkness.

Question 7 - Drinking and Driving

(D) The type of alcohol does not affect blood alcohol concentration, as standard servings of different types of alcohol contain the same amount of alcohol.

Question 8 - Drinking and Driving

(D) Even small amounts of alcohol can impair a driver's reflexes, driving skills, and depth perception.

Question 9 - Drinking and Driving

(D) License suspension is mandatory for minors convicted of driving under the influence of drugs or transporting an open container of any alcoholic beverage.

Question 10 - Drinking and Driving

(B) Drunk driving is the leading cause of death among young Americans aged 16 to 24, with alcohol-related crashes occurring every 33 minutes.

Question 11 - Drinking and Driving

(D) Open containers of alcohol are only allowed in areas inaccessible to drivers or passengers, such as trunks, cargo areas, or truck beds.

Question 12 - Drinking and Driving

(D) Alcohol can impact your concentration, reaction time, and judgment.

Question 13 - Drinking and Driving

(D) Consuming alcohol before or while driving can diminish a driver's reflexes, physical control of the vehicle, and awareness of potential dangers on the road.

Question 14 - Drinking and Driving

(A) Drivers under 21 are not permitted to buy, consume, or possess alcohol.

Question 15 - Drinking and Driving

(A) The liver can process approximately one standard drink per hour. If you consume a large amount of alcohol, it may take a day or two for your body to fully recover.

Question 16 - Drinking and Driving

(A) Open container laws prohibit open containers of alcohol in areas accessible to the driver or passengers of a vehicle, with exceptions for limousines, taxis, motor homes, and commercial buses.

Question 17 - Drinking and Driving

(D) If you plan to drink alcohol, consider using public transportation, a taxi, or designating a sober driver to get home safely.

Question 18 - Drinking and Driving

(D) Drivers under the influence of alcohol are more likely to drive too fast or too slow, change lanes frequently, and fail to dim headlights.

Question 19 - Drinking and Driving

(D) For minors between the ages of 15 and 21, it is illegal to possess, consume, attempt to purchase, or purchase alcohol, or have a BAC of 0.02% or higher.

Question 20 - Drinking and Driving

(D) Alcohol enters the bloodstream and affects various bodily processes, such as coordination, self-control, and reaction time. The only way to counteract alcohol's impact on the brain is to wait for it to leave the bloodstream.

EXAM TEST PRACTICE

.

Question 1 - Mock Exam

(C) If you feel like your tires are losing traction with the road, your first course of action should be to reduce your speed by lifting your foot off the gas pedal. Simultaneously, you should aim to keep the steering wheel as steady as possible. Avoid abrupt stops or turns until your tires regain traction. If you absolutely need to make a turn, do so gently to avoid causing a skid.

Question 2 - Mock Exam

(B) When overtaking a large truck or commercial vehicle, drivers should be wary of the truck's No-Zones. These are large blind spots that exist on the front, rear, and sides of the truck. While it may not be possible to completely steer clear of these zones, it's crucial to spend as little time in them as possible while passing.

Question 3 - Mock Exam

(A) On roads with multiple lanes, the leftmost lane is traditionally used for passing slower vehicles. Passing on the right could be risky, as the other driver may not see you and might unexpectedly change lanes.

Question 4 - Mock Exam

(C) U-turns are not only dangerous but also illegal in certain situations, such as on divided highways, near the top of a hill or in curves, and at railroad crossings. Making a U-turn in these locations could result in an accident.

Question 5 - Mock Exam

(A) Aggressive driving behaviors, such as repeatedly flashing headlights, can lead to unsafe situations on the road. If you find yourself in this situation, the best response is to avoid engaging the other driver and move out of the way when it's safe to do so.

Question 6 - Mock Exam

(A) When you're on a single-lane or two-lane road and come to an intersection with a divided highway or a road with three or more lanes, you are required to yield the right-of-way to the traffic on the main road.

Question 7 - Mock Exam

(C) Two solid yellow lines usually indicate a no-passing zone. Crossing these lines is generally prohibited except when making a left turn. However, California law provides an exception: if you're in a carpool or HOV lane with a designated left-side entrance, you may drive to the left of these lines.

Question 8 - Mock Exam

(C) In California, you're permitted to make a U-turn at an intersection, within a residential district, or through a specially designed opening in the median or barrier of a divided highway.

Question 9 - Mock Exam

(A) To avoid skidding, it's advised to slow down before entering a curve, thus avoiding the need to brake while you're in the curve. Braking during a turn can cause your vehicle to skid.

Question 10 - Mock Exam

(B) Double solid yellow lines on the road signify a no-passing zone. Therefore, crossing these lines to overtake another vehicle is generally not permitted.

Question 11 - Mock Exam

(C) If you are not matching the speed of the surrounding vehicles, it is best to stay in the lane closest to the right side of the road. However, always adhere to the speed limits.

Question 12 - Mock Exam

(B) Double parking, which involves parking your car on the street in front of another vehicle when all legal parking spots at the curb are occupied, is illegal in California and in most other states.

Question 13 - Mock Exam

(C) "NEV Use Only" lanes are intended for Neighborhood Electric Vehicles (NEVs) and other low-speed vehicles (LSVs). These vehicles are battery-powered and travel at slow speeds (25 mph or less) and are prohibited from operating on roadways with a speed limit exceeding 35 mph.

Question 14 - Mock Exam

(A) When parking your vehicle on a level street, the tires should be positioned parallel to the curb.

Question 15 - Mock Exam

(B) You can lightly tap your horn to establish eye contact with another driver. Nevertheless, your horn should not be used to express frustration or criticize other drivers.

Question 16 - Mock Exam

(B) Emotions can significantly impact your driving. Avoid letting your emotions interfere with safe driving. Follow the recommended safe driving rules and avoid driving when you're upset or angry.

Question 17 - Mock Exam

(C) When you approach an intersection, adhere to the left-right-left rule: Look to your left first as vehicles from the left are closer to you. Then look to your right, and finally, look to your left again before you proceed. You may spot a vehicle on your left that you didn't notice when you first looked.

Question 18 - Mock Exam

(C) Before reaching the freeway exit, you should signal at least 5 seconds in advance to prepare to leave the freeway.

Question 19 - Mock Exam

(C) If you need to cross several lanes on the freeway, it is safest to cross them one at a time.

Question 20 - Mock Exam

(C) In California, it is illegal to drive off the paved or main-traveled portion of the road or on the shoulder for the purpose of overtaking another vehicle on the right.

Question 21 - Mock Exam

(A) When kids are present around a school, the speed limit within a distance of 500–1000 feet is reduced to 25 mph.

Question 22 - Mock Exam

(C) Stopping next to a white curb is allowed, but only for a brief period necessary to pick up or drop off passengers or mail. Freight loading or unloading is not permitted.

Question 23 - Mock Exam

(B) When you're planning to make a turn, it's crucial to signal your intent well before the turn. Under California law, drivers intending to turn must start signaling at least 100 feet prior to the turn, even if no other vehicles are visible.

Question 24 - Mock Exam

(C) If the weather conditions require the use of your windshield wipers, you are also obligated to turn on your vehicle's headlights.

Question 25 - Mock Exam

(C) The large size of tractor-trailers can make them appear to be moving slower than their actual speed. Be careful when passing or turning not to underestimate their speed or proximity.

Question 26 - Mock Exam

(A) The maximum distance you can travel in a center left-turn lane is 200 feet. This lane is not intended for passing.

Question 27 - Mock Exam

(C) In California, you can make a left turn against a red light only when turning from a one-way street onto another one-way street. However, laws about left turns on red may differ in other states.

Question 28 - Mock Exam

(B) Before changing lanes or turning, make sure to check over your shoulder for motorcycles. Due to their smaller size, they can be more difficult to spot.

Question 29 - Mock Exam

(B) In California, U-turns in a business district on an undivided roadway are only legal at intersections or through a designated opening in a barrier or median. It's important to note that, in California, business districts include areas with churches, apartments, multifamily housing units, or public buildings, excluding schools.

Question 30 - Mock Exam

(B) As of January 1, 2023, when overtaking a bicyclist, you're required to move into another lane going in your direction, if possible. If there's no available lane, you must provide at least three feet of space between your vehicle and the bicycle.

Question 31 - Mock Exam

(A) To ensure timely reaction to road situations, it's crucial to scan the road 10–15 seconds ahead of your vehicle rather than focusing solely on the car right in front. Keep checking your surroundings and use your mirrors to understand what's happening behind you as well.

Question 32 - Mock Exam

(C) It's always safer to maintain a larger following distance when dealing with potentially risky drivers or vehicles. So, increase your distance when the driver behind wishes to pass or if the vehicle ahead is large or heavy. Also, during adverse road conditions, such as slippery roads, it's wise to maintain extra distance.

Question 33 - Mock Exam

(B) Steering with one hand is only recommended when you're reversing or when you need to operate other vehicle controls.

Question 34 - Mock Exam

(C) When merging into freeway traffic, the vehicles already on the freeway have the right-of-way.

Question 35 - Mock Exam

(C) In work (cone) zones, it's best to slow down, increase your following distance, minimize distractions, and stay vigilant for sudden stoppages. Avoid unnecessary attention diversion.

Question 36 - Mock Exam

(B) To avoid sudden maneuvers, aim to look down the road 10–15 seconds ahead of your vehicle.

Question 37 - Mock Exam

(C) When reentering traffic from a parked position, it's the vehicles already on the road that have the right-of-way.

Question 38 - Mock Exam

(B) Avoid entering an intersection if you cannot fully clear it before the light turns red. Blocking an intersection can lead to penalties.

Question 39 - Mock Exam

(A) If you're 18 or older, you can use your cell phone while driving only if it's a hands-free device.

Question 40 - Mock Exam

(B) Don't follow within 300 feet of any emergency vehicle with a siren or flashing lights, which is about the length of a football

Question 41 - Mock Exam

(B) You should only overtake another vehicle when approaching a curve or a hill if it is safe to do so. Check for road conditions and other traffic that might force other vehicles into your lane before you pass.

Question 42 - Mock Exam

(B) When there are three or more lanes in one direction, the middle lanes typically offer the smoothest flow of traffic. The left lane is for those who wish to go faster, overtake, or turn left. The right lane should be used by slower vehicles and those intending to turn right.

Question 43 - Mock Exam

(B) If your vehicle breaks down and you can't get it entirely off the road, stop where your vehicle can be clearly seen from behind.

Question 44 - Mock Exam

(A) The vehicle moving downhill should yield the right-of-way because it has better control.

Question 45 - Mock Exam

(A) Before changing lanes on a freeway, it's recommended that you signal for at least 5 seconds.

Question 46 - Mock Exam

(B) If you notice a vehicle ahead with both right and left turn signals flashing, it means the vehicle has turned on its hazard lights (emergency flashers). Slow down as the vehicle might be experiencing mechanical issues, or there might be a collision or other road emergency ahead. Offer assistance if asked or pass very cautiously.

A MESSAGE FROM THE DRIVING SCHOOL

As we wrap up this workbook, we just wanted to say a big thank you! We're so glad you chose us to be a part of your journey towards mastering the art of driving. It's been an absolute pleasure helping you get closer to acing that DMV exam.

We genuinely care about your success and satisfaction, and we're always looking for ways to make our resources better. That's where you come in - we'd love to hear your thoughts about this workbook.

Your feedback is like gold dust to us. It not only helps us improve, but it also guides future learners who are just starting out on their driving journey. So, if you have a spare moment, would you mind sharing your experience with this workbook?

Leaving a review is easy as pie. Just head over to where you bought the book and let us know what you think. Every single word you share matters to us, and we're really excited to hear about your learning journey.

Once again, a big thank you for picking our workbook. We're cheering you on and wishing you all the best as you hit the road and put all that learning into action. Safe driving and take care!

Thank you so much,

Drive Ready Publications

Made in United States
Troutdale, OR
08/28/2023